TECHNICAL EDUCATION IN NORTH-EAST INDIA

Sunanda Datta

RAJESH PUBLICATIONS
NEW DELHI-110 002

First Published in India : 1998
ISBN : 81-85891-18-4

Published by :
M.L. Gupta
RAJESH PUBLICATIONS
1, Ansari Road, Darya Ganj,
New Delhi - 110 002

Type Setter :
Anita Gupta
SANJAY ENTERPRISES
New Delhi-110 002

Printed at :
GRAPHIC PRINT
New Delhi-110 002.

Contents

Preface

Technical Education of a country looks in two directions : it reflects the stage of technical capability available in the country; it further reflects the direction which a country wishes to follow for its economic and material welfare. The present book is an attempt to record these two aspects of technical education as it pertains to India in general and the North-East in particular.

North East India as a whole, the "Seven Sisters" to be precise, is rich in natural and human resources. However, the means to translate these into economic prosperity and material comforts and facilities for the region are at a stage where minimal utilisation is made and a rapid depletion of resources takes place. In other words, what is taken out, is not put back, so that rejuvenation of resources is not an acceptable automatic process. Hence the technological process is not a self-sustainable one. To my mind this reflects the thinking related to technical education, the means at our disposal to improve our lot.

In the book an attempt is made to explore the reason why this should be so. Obviously, there are historical reasons. Further, it involves locating technical education within science education and analysing science policy decisions as a whole. It means considering the goals of technical education within a particular socio-political and economic milieu, considering the means for implementing these and checking whether these are working in actuality, since policy decisions neither translate automatically into actuality nor do they take root in the environment as a matter of course. It thus also means looking at the total context where technical education has to work : whether it grows out of the social context or whether it is an imposition at contradiction with the context. The tensions or their absence will influence the failure or success of technical education within a particular society. As such then, technical education is a part of a socio-economic process; it influences and is in turn influenced by society.

Hence understanding the attitudes of all the participants in technical education, learners, teachers, parents, employees and employers is an essential part of policy making decisions. The extent to which these are considered would influence the nature of such education and would determine the nature of the end product : technical personnel.

5, Broad Street
Calcutta - 700019

Dr. Sunanda Datta

1

Introduction

The technical education of a country looks in two directions. On the one hand it reflects the state of technical capability or the degree of industrialisation available in the country. On the other hand it reflects the direction which a country or a nation wishes to follow for its future economie and material welfare. As a developing country, India as a whole is caught just in the position where it "looks before and after, and pines for what is not". Within India, the North-East region as a gegoraphical unit, displays certain common social, economic and political features. How these relate to the concept of technical education and what impact technical education is likely to have on the region and its people are areas which have not always been studied in depth.

The present book makes an attempt to define technical education in the Indian context, consider how technical education has evolved with changes in society and what demands it makes on its learners in particular and on society as a whole.

India has the distinction of possessing one of the largest pools of scientific and technical personnel in the world. However, India is not considered to be a very highly industrialised country. There seems to be an anomaly here. Such an anomaly may have several causes and may be the outcome of a faulty system of technical education. Other causes may be disparate development, disparate distribution of resources and facilities, inappropriate planning, non-relevant technology and the like.

Another aspect which needs to be taken into account is the amount of fit between technical education and the social fabric. Like the Indian education system as a whole, technical education in India has not been an indigenous growth, geared to the needs and aspirations of the people of India, but has been imported from the West to cater to the material needs of the rulers and their empire-building activities. This means that along with the content of technical education, attendant beliefs and attitudes have also been brought over.

When a particular society develops a system, that system is attuned to the values and the particular needs of that society. If the system is transplanted , that attunement need not necessarily get transferred. In such a case mutual sustenance between the system and the receiving society may not develop at all. If such is the case, the system remains weak and needs regeneration from time to time. The analogy is that of a potted plant as compared to a plant growing in the soil. It is within the bounds of possibility that technical education in India is of such a nature and that may be the reason why with the third largest body of technical personnel in the world, India is still one among the under industrialised nations.

The further point that needs to be made is that the kind of machine - intensive heavy industries model imported from the West may not be the appropriate one for a country like India which is basically agricultural and which is immensely rich in human and natural resources.

Moreover, it is becoming increasingly clear that traditional industries play havoc with the environment and deplete natural resources beyond repair. In addition, such industries are not at all environment-friendly and pollute air, water and soil, causing diseases of various kinds and weakening the human potential. Hence there is a pressing need for evolving a kind of technical education which takes into account the emerging concerns of society. In other words, technical education needs to be flexible, sensitive to the changes taking place in society and amenable to the value bases of society. It has to be able to sustain itself and sustain the society in which it operates. The needs of the society will shape its nature and it will in turn regulate the society in a number of ways.

Further, technical education is usually seen as an instrument of development and change. However, the concept of "development" is a changing one and is indeed being redefined during the nineties. Development does not necessarily mean a high GNP, good roads, concrete houses, possession of T.V. and cars, or a life-style using/wasting large amounts of natural resources. Recently the concept of development has been redefined as "sustainable economic development" in the face of an imminent environmental and social catastrophe. Thus it has become imperative to re-orient the present life style and attitude to the use of the natural resources base. This means that within differing contexts development will manifest itself in differing ways, and no single model will be appropriate for all contexts. As Ghosh (1996) has pointed out,

> "`Sustainable economic development' in the wider connotation, indicates the socio-economic and cultural developmental path for both industrialised and developing countries. It is to be conceived meaningfully as a problem for the human civilisation on the aggregative level, for the present generation as well as in the intergenerational context."
>
> **(Ghosh 1996 : 49)**

The cultural and social aspects of technical education thus assume a great significance. In fact, international funding agencies are becoming increasingly aware of the fact that development projects work best when these fit in with the life style of the receiving group and are sustained by them. For instance, the current trend of rising population in India, with a given level of technology, generates immense pressure on its natural resource base and available economic opportunities. The existing level of resources will have to be spread very thin unless alternative strategies for either genrating more resources or finding alternative ones are formulated. This calls for a drastically different policy formulation rather than strengthening the existing ones. This need not be the case in relation to developed countries where population growth is either zero or even negative. The type of technology favoured by such countries is likely to be machine/automation oriented rather than labour intensive. In a country like India on the other hand, abundance of labour demands a type of technology which can utilise human labour to the fullest extent. This would suggest cottage industry and small scale industries rather than heavy industries being the appropriate modes of technology for India.

In order to put into perspective the ways in which technical education operates in India at present, we need to consider the origin and history of technical and vocational education in India. Since technical education studies consist of the applied aspects of the findings of science, the history of technical and vocational education cannot be separated from that of science education. The following account of science education in India will attempt to bring out the factors which influenced the decision-making processes. In the account that follows, we will be looking at the historical changes in the goals of science education in India and the consequences of these changes on the curriculum and instruction in technical education.

Historical changes in the goals and programmes of science education raises several fundamental questions. Some of these are : How does science education change ? What, in fact, changes in science education ? When does science education change ? Why does science education change ? Moreover, in order to be seen in its proper perspective, science education must be considered within the total context of general education. The basic question that can be formulated is : Are there identifiable goals which have continually been a part of science education ?If these goals do exist, then there is the further question, do variations in the goals result in different models of science curriculum and instruction ? There is the further hypothesis that the aims and models would have changed in different directions due to varying social forces and that these changes would be recognizable upon analysis. In general then, the organization of curriculum and instruction in science education is influenced by three major goals : the *knowledge* of science, the *methods* of science and the *development* of the individual. First, there is the modification or updating of the goals, since in science knowledge is always expanding and existing theories undergoing changes in the light of new knowledge. Secondly, there is a short-term reorganization in the order of priority given to the individual goals. Is it knowledge, for example, or is it the method of science, which should have priority ? Third, goals ascend or descend in organizational prominence over a longer period of time. Such changes are related to social forces which operate at a particular point of time within a particular society. Further, the goals are modified from within science education while the organization and context of the specifc aims in models of curriculum and instruction are largely influenced by societal and scientific changes. Goals of science education and societal changes thus form the two bases of a curriculum related to science education, as set out in Fig. 1.1.

Science education, in its turn, is influenced by the discoveries of science, and the state of knowledge in science at any given point of time. On the other hand, societal changes are related to the economic development, cultural traditions and the relationships between a particular society and technological changes. The last takes into account how technologically oriented a particular society is. These factors are set out in a diagrammatical form in Fig. 1.2.

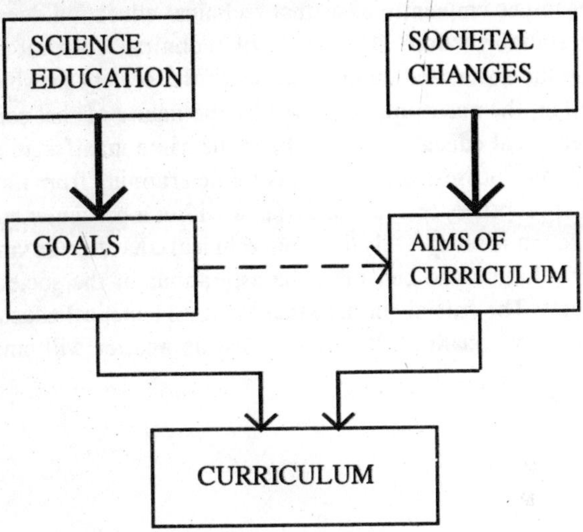

Fig.1.1 Bases of the curriculum : First approximation

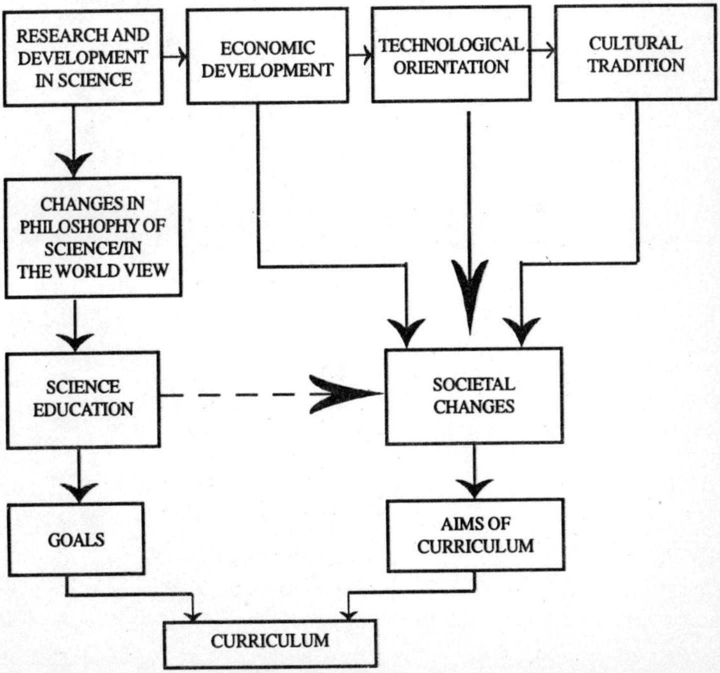

Fig. 1.2. Bases of the curriculum : Second approximation

It thus becomes eminently clear that technical education does not operate in a social vacuum. The goals of technical education are determined by the social and cultural norms of the society in which it operates. Further, the needs are generated by the nature of that society itself. Thus technical education cannot have the same manifestation in all contexts. It must possess the modalities for determining from time to time, what is appropriate, relevant and viable within a particular socio-cultural and economic set up. Only then can technical education be vibrant and dynamic in nature and can fulfil the aspirations of the society in which it operates. The crucial question thus is : does technical education in India possess this quality ? It is hoped that an answer will emerge subsequently.

2

Technical Education in British India

Though ancient India has been rich in technological tradition as its gun making and iron works testify to, the present day technical education is a consequence of British Colonial rule, and not a continuation of its earlier heritage. This means that the needs for technical education did not emerge from the society itself but arose out of the perception the rulers had for the management of that society. It is quiet conceivable that the interests of the two groups were in conflict or the two systems (the society and imported technical education) were incompatible. If that is so, the conflict or incompatability will manifest itself in some way or the other. To understand what was actually happening, it is necessary to consider technical education from a historical perspective.

Historical Background :

Technical education in India is a legacy of British rule. Its nature and evolution can be understood fully only when it is seen in a historical perspective. The concept of technical education and the content of such education in India was initially shaped by empire building processes. The very concept of such education further reflected the British view as it was current at the time. To understand why technician education today is of the kind it is, it is necessary to look at the historical processes through which it has evolved. This historical perspective is provided by the numerous letters, memos, despatches, resolutions and reports generated in British India and the subsequent policy on scientific and technical education in post independent India. One aspect of the plethora of these materials needs special mention. Often the aims envisaged were set out clearly, but the machinery for implementing these were not spelt out. As a result we find document after document advocating the same kind of aims over a number of years, the implication being that what was specified earlier, has not been achieved. For example, between the years 1886 and 1907, a period of twenty years or so, at least fourteen such documents had been generated. The Sadler Commission (1917) however, dismissed most of this material as being "largely infructious". Indeed it is true to say that there is probably no other subject on which more had been written or said, while less had been accomplished. The scene did not change much till the independence of India, when a more integrated view of technical education was adopted. Such abundance of recommendations and proposals is matched by extremely scanty material on what exact concrete steps were taken to implement the recommended measures. In fact, till 1917 it is difficult to reconstruct with any certainty, an authentic account of courses studied, books used and methods of instruction utilised in all the institutions in existence. Because of the detailed documentation of reports, recommendations and opinion, the Sadler Commission provides an indirect picture of technical and vocational education upto that time. Abbott and Wood's report on technical education (1937) makes several concrete proposals which in themselves indicate the actual state of such education. Documents such as these two reveal the foundations on which technical curriculum in India is based. They state and clarify the issues, make decisions of one kind or another, providing a rationale for doing so. The historical perspective thus provides not only an account of the sequence of events but an insight into the forces which have gone into the thinking behind the proposals and recommendations made. It is with such forces that the present chapter is concerned.

In post-independent India this historical legacy has been modified by current thinking in developmental education, and by the changed goals of economic and social growth. These forces have then acted as the bases for syllabus design.

Educational Policy Under Company Rule (1813-1858) :

1813 marks the beginning of a formal education policy for India under the British rule. From this date to 1858 we find the thrust of the subsequent policies changing direction in significant ways. Such changes emanated from the overall Indo-British relationship prevalent at the time. During the half century or so under consideration, it passed through three consecutive phases, namely (a) the conservative attitude; (b) the liberal, evangelical and the utilitarian attitude; and (c) the imperial or the colonial attitude (Stokes 1959; Bearce 1961; Ashby 1966). These are exemplified in the Charter Act of 1813, Macaulay's Minute and Wood's Despatch respectively. In this chapter the impact of these policies on education in India will be discussed and interpreted.

The Charter Act of 1813 :

Section 43 of the Charter Act of the East India Company set aside of a sum of one lakh of rupees annually for two very diverse objectives : the "revival and improvement of literature and the encouragement of the learned natives of India" and for "the introduction and promotion of a knowledge of science among the inhabitants of the British territories in India".

We will now consider some of the features of this Act. First of all, the company did not assume any responsibility for educating Indians on a large scale. This is not surprising, since trading companies can hardly be expected to educate those they do trade with. Secondly, it set up a duality within education, which persisted subsequently. The study of literature was considered as distinct from the "knowledge of science". There was the implication that such knowledge did not exist among the natives of India and that this knowledge was considered essential for them. Third, education was separated from religion of any kind. Fourth, though the act was enacted in 1813, it was not until 1823 that it began to be implemented.

Further, it was not made clear what the "knowledge of science" mentioned in the second part of the act might mean, and hence no formal steps were taken in this direction. However, it appears (from the account in the Radhakrishnan Report, 1948-49) that by 1825, technical schools were in operation in Bombay and Calcutta. These trained personnel like overseers needed to construct and maintain public buildings, roads, canals and ports; and artisans and craftsmen needed to produce instruments and apparatus for use in the army, navy and the survey departments. Their skills were developed through practical work. The majority of the trainees were the sons of artisans and lacked literacy. It can thus be safely assumed that the languages used for imparting such skills were the mother tongues of the trainees. However, there was no explicitly formulated policy on technical education in the years following the Act.

Macaulay's Minute (1835) :

The immediate purpose of the Minute was to put an end to the controversy raging within the General Committee of Public Instruction in India over the promotion of oriental languages and literature. In the process Macaulay argues eloquently for an Western education imparted through English.

Macaulay denigrates oriental and Indian languages and their literature, and as a conrollary, the moral and intellectual character of the entire nation. Consequently he envisages a kind of renaissance for the Indians, by rejecting whatever kind of education they had, and by substituting an English education in its place.

For such a purpose Macaulay advocates that the extension of education be restricted to the upper classes who have leisure for study, and whose culture would later filter down to the masses. The content would be western knowledge, including the study of science. In order to justify the claim of English as the medium of instruction, Macaulay advances a number of arguments, consisting of a very mixed bag of criteria like status, power, communicative worth and utility. He saw no reason for making any special provision for the teaching of English to Indian students before it could be used as the medium of instruction.

Science was treated on a par with subjects like literature, history or jurisprudence. The criterion for inclusion was utility, but the kind of knowledge of science needed was not specified in any way. Nor was technical education specifically or explicitly mentioned. This is not entirely surprising since at the time apart from training men to be ordained into the anglican church, the English universities did not serve as gateways into the professions. Science was not part of the curriculum in these universities and were not considered fit subjects for academic disciplines.[1] In the context of the Minute, the knowledge of science could not thus have meant any academic discipline or subject. In the perspective of the industrial revolution that had already taken place in England, a knowledge of science could have referred either to a knowledge of practical skills or to the application of the principles of science for controlling the environment in various ways, that is, what would now-a-days be termed as technology or technical knowledge. Whatever Macaulay might have meant, his minute did not specify any particular measures which could be adopted for implementing what he was suggesting. In the absence of any official policy on technical education, the technical schools already in operation went their own ways, developing according to the demands of the situation.

Education Despatch of 1854 (Wood's Despatch) :

> The purported purpose of this document was to confer "---- upon the natives of India those vast moral and material blessings which flow from the general diffusion of *useful knowledge*".
>
> ***(Despatch 1854, para 2; my emphasis)***

The despatch clearly sees the material advantages related to education. Though the content of this education is not spelt out in any detail, the aim is clear : help in the increase of trade and commerce by ensuring supply of raw materials from India for manufacture in England and by providing a market for the finished products. European knowledge is considered necessary to develop the resources of India. This is surely vocational education and technical in nature. A second strand of vocational education is envisaged when education is expected to supply the administration "with servants to whose probity" one may "with increased confidence commit offices of trust". It appears that the Despatch, though it does not claim to do so, is really advocating vocational and technical education.

Wood makes a further distinction between the learning of a less high order and "high attainment in English literature and European sciences" by Indians. A small number of people, drawn from the "higher classes" are to be given the opportunity "for the acquisition of a liberal European education", whereas for the rest only "useful and practical knowledge" is suitable. This can be seen as a fundamental distinction made between training and education.[2] The higher education was to be imparted through English while the useful arts could be transmitted only through the vernaculars. Wood thus associates vocational training with vernacular languages and *not* with English.

This view of practical arts (referring to both scientific and technical education) as being "more suitable for artisans and the lower middle classes than for the governing classes" prevented technical education from gaining the kind of prestige that was associated with a literary education with its concept of a liberalising influence, and had led to its subsequent unpopularity with the upper middle classes.

The Universities Act of 1857 :

While planning the curriculum for the proposed university of Calcutta, the committee set up for the purpose made provisions for a degree in civil engineering along with degrees in arts, law and medicine. This appears to be the first instance of official educational policy regarding technical education.

An Overview :

Macaulay's Minute helped establish secular "English Education" in India. It was meant for a small group of people and though it mentions the study of sciences and that education should be useful, there is no explicit reference to the kind of technical and vocational education that could be instituted for the Indians. In contrast, Wood's Despatch refers to the various kinds of practical training that was already available, and those which could be set up. It stresses the importance of vocational instruction and to that end, the need for establishing vocational colleges and schools of industry. It was suggested that existing schools could provide more opportunities for such education. It recommends the proposition for attaching a branch for teaching practical agriculture to each Zilla School (Wood 1854 : 20). The Despatch also proposed the establishment of training schools for schoolmasters to combat the inadequate supply of qualified schoolmasters and improve an imperfect method of teaching (Ibid p.16). For technical education, civil engineering was seen to be of special importance. Wood praises the success of the Thomason College of Civil Engineering at Roorkee, established in 1847, where instruction was of a practical nature, qualifying the natives of India for employment in the rapidly expanding system of railways and public works, thus providing personnel for government works. There was a constant growing demand for such people and openings existed for a large number of persons. Wood suggests that "it is expedient that similar places for practical instruction in civil engineering should be established in other parts of India" (p.20). Along with these, medical colleges and schools of industry and design are to be set up as "institutions of an essentially practical character".

As we have already mentioned, the thinking behind maintaining the dichotomy in education by class and languages (liberal education and English for the higher classes and practical training through the vernacular for the masses), as advocated in Wood's Despatch, can be understood if we consider the concepts of society and education in the England of the time. The belief in the fixed order of society was responsible for considering liberal education as the birth-right of the upper classes whereas the lower classes were concerned with manual labour and crafts. These notions were imported to India along with the educational policies framed in England (Ashby 1966a). Moreover, the aims of the practical training envisaged for Indians were limited and narrowly defined. The technical education as it existed and as it was proposed, were strictly need-based, of a narrow kind, and not governed by any philosophy of education. It must be pointed out that the reason for such a "narrow" view of technical and vocational education lies not solely in the "empire-building" activities but in the Englishman's attitude to science education. The study of science, even in England at the time, was characterised by the absence of a philosophical attitude (Ashby 1966a). In the 1850's and the 1860's scientific education began in the schools and universities of England, not because it was the main stream of European thought[3], but because it would improve the efficiency of manufacture. Such a pragmatic attitude led to scientific education being regarded "as more suitable for artisans and the lower middle classes than for the governing classes". (Ashby 1966a : 31). And of course, associated with this was the notion persisting in Britain at the time that the content of higher education should be stratified according to class, a notion deeply embedded in the minds of some of the men who had to shape Britain's policy for education overseas (Ibid : 22). It is not surprising then, that when technical education was imported into India, with these attendant attitudes, the upper classes receiving English education found it unacceptable[4]. In addition, even the so called liberal education for the upper classes as envisaged in the Despatch has been criticised on the following grounds :

> "---- the authors of the Despatch did not aim at education for leadership, education for the industrial regeneration of India, education for the defence of the motherland, in short, education required by the people of a self-government nation".
>
> ***(Paranjpe, 1941)***

In 1858 the East India Company ceased to be a political power and the Government came directly under the Crown. Thus the Despatch was the last policy on education under company rule. However, the guidelines laid down in that document continued to influence education in India for a long time to come. Secondly, we see both from the Minute and the Despatch how cultural and social norms influence the goals of education. This is shown diagrammatically in Fig. 2.1.

Education Policy Under the Crown : 1859 - 1919 :

In the period immediately after India was taken over by the Crown,

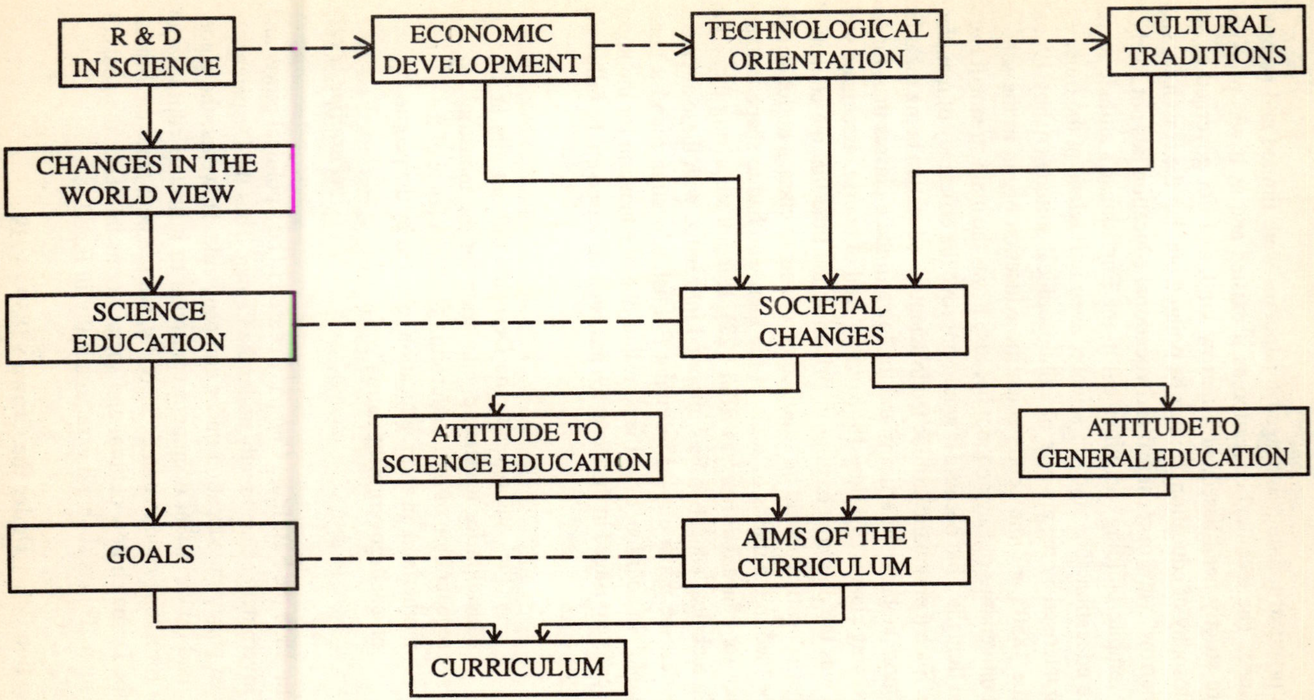

Fig. 2.1 Bases of the Curriculum : Third Approximation

no drastic change in educational policy occurred. The resolutions, reports of commissions and conferences, and acts either implemented the policies already undertaken, or were geared to offsetting what were seen as defects in the system that existed. Things were more or less allowed to take their own course, though voices of concern were raised now and then. A decisive step was taken when the Calcutta University Commission was set up in 1917 under the chairmanship of Michael Sadler, to look into the whole question of education in India.

Indian Education Commission 1882-83 :

Though the Commission was precluded from studying professional colleges, it gave considerable attention to the provision of vocational courses at the upper secondary stage with a view to preparing pupils for various walks of life. It recommended a bifurcation of the secondary course and the provision for alternative examinations in every state. Following these recommendations, question papers for alternative examinations began to be set in a number of states, but no provision was made for teaching the courses. It is not surprising then, that these examinations were not very popular. Some time later this lack of popularity was advanced as the reason for discontinuing the examinations and the lack of enthusiasm was seen as a typical example of Indian apathy to techincal education.

Technical Education between 1883 and 1915 :

A Government of India Resolution issued in 1886 pointed out the "little progress of substantial character" that had been achieved since 1857 in technical education in India. Sir. A.P. MacDonnel's *Memorandum on Technical Education in India prior to 1886*, dated 23rd July, 1886, dealt with the inherent weaknesses of the system. He considered the industrial schools in Bengal as "mere excrescences on the educational system with neither plan nor subject". Acting on the basis of these two reports, the Government of India issued a Resolution in 1888, recommending that an industrial survey be held for each of the provinces of Bengal, Bombay and Madras. The survey for Bengal[5] was made in 1890 by Mr. E.W. Collin. In the same year Sir A.Colvin wrote a Minute on Technical Education. Mr. J.S. Cotton, writing the third Quinquennial Review of Progress of Education in India[6] for the years 1893-87, remarked that there seems to be "no appearance of a system of technical education anywhere" in India, except, perhaps, in Madras. In the next review for 1898-1902, Mr. Nathan was constrained to admit that endeavours made to provide a system of technical education in India had met with little success. In 1901 there was an inauguration of a fresh cycle of enquiry, discussion and investigation. Sir Edward Buck's report on *Practical and Technical Education* (1901) was considered at the Simla educational conference of 1901. In 1903, a Commission on Industrial Education submitted its report in two parts. Schemes and proposals for improving technical education were made by Sir A. Pedlar, the then Director of Public Instruction of Bengal, in 1903, and by the Association for Advancement of Scientific and Industrial Education in 1905. K.D. Bhargava, reviewing the whole scene, remarks rightly :

> "There is probably no subject on which more had been written or said, while less had been accomplished".
>
> ***(1968 : 1)***

The Calcutta University Commission (1917-19) however, described all this pen-pushing in much stronger terms, as "voluminous, suggestive but comparatively infructious" (Vol. 3; 154).

These documents serve one purpose at least, even if they do not bring about any change : they provide us with a picture of what technical education was like during the period. It appears that the Industrial schools that functioned in the various provinces, trained pupils to develop the necessary skills through practical work. The majority of the trainees were the sons of artisans and lacked literacy. In order to increase the efficiency of these trainees, some of the schools made arrangements for imparting the skills of reading and writing, and the principles of arithmetic, geometry and mechanics, usually outside normal hours of work. The earliest engineering institution in India was founded in Bombay prior to 1824[7], and was maintained wholly at government expense. In 1824 it had 36 Indians and 14 lads of mixed descent. By 1826 the number rose to 86 (Sharp 1920, Vol. 1 : 78). The subsequent history of this institution is obscure (Richey 1920, Vol. II : 350). In 1844 a class for training engineers was opened in the Elphinestone Institution, but for want of suitable candidates, was discontinued in 1847. In Madras at Guindy, an interesting industrial school for ordinance Artificers was opened in 1840[8] by Major Maitland, Superintendent of the Gun Carriage Manufactory. A school of Industrial Arts was opened by Dr. Hunter in Madras in 1850. In Poona, a school for overseers existed in 1854. A training school for overseers, started in 1845 in Roorkee in the North Western Provinces, became the Thomason Civil Engineering College in

1847, the first such college to be established in India. By 1856, three colleges of engineering had been set up in the three presidencies of Bengal, Bombay and Madras. Of these, the Calcutta College, called the Bengal Engineering College, was later shifted to Sibpur. For some reason, the Bombay scheme failed and the Poona school became the Poona College of Engineering. In Madras, the school of engineering in Guindy became the Guindy college of Engineering. Similar work was done by all the three institutions : till 1880, they ran licentiate courses in civil engineering. After that date degree classes began to be conducted. For electrical and mechanical engineering, degree classes did not begin till the 1930's. The National Council of Education organised by the Swadeshi movement attempted to set up a national university in 1907. The College of Engineering and Technology in Jadavpur survived, and started granting diplomas in a mechanical and engineering courses in 1908.

The Indian Universities Commission set up in 1902 at the instance of Lord Curzon, proposed an extended role for the universities in practical studies. It deplored the want of higher agricultural training in a country so predominently agricultural as India. It thought that the most appropriate training would be a two-part course : a period of mainly theoretical study in college, followed by a period of practical work on the farms. The Commission also commented upon the neglect of suitable training for those willing to follow a commercial career. It did not think that the time had come for introducing degree work in commerce, and suggested that universities should encourage commercial pursuits as far as possible. Lord Curzon enunciated a new policy for agricultural education. He organised the Agricultural Departments, created the Central Research Institute at Pusa and laid down the principle that every important province in India must have its own Agricultural College. He also proposed the introduction of agriculture as a subject at the Middle and High school stages and the conducting of special classes for the training of agriculturists. Lord Curzon instituted a number of scholarships to encourage Indian students to study technology abroad.

Two more documents need to be mentioned in relation to technical education. The first is the proposal for the setting up of a university at Dacca, made in 1912. It suggested the setting up of an engineering department within it. The other is the Indian Industrial Commission for the development of engineering education in India, set up in 1915. This recommended the creation of an Institution of Engineers in India.

The Calcutta University Commission : 1917-19 (Sadler Report) and Technical Education :

The Calcutta University Commission, set up in 1917 primarily "to enquire into the condition and prospects of the University of Calcutta----" (Report 1919, Vol I : 1), sought to give their recommendations a general validity by framing them against the background of the total university system. The commission's essential criticism of the existing curriculum was that it was too predominantly literary in character, too narrow in scope, too uniform and stereotyped (Ibid I : 380; 397 ff; IV : 13-15; V : 302). As a result it was "out of touch with the requirements of modern life" and catered ineffectively for the contemporary needs of the country. In order to remedy the situation, the commission recommended a bold expansion of the facilities for professional, vocational and technological training and a substantial improvement in teacher training.

After reviewing the existing conditions in technical education, the commission recommended a high grade and a lower grade within it. Degree courses in agriculture, consisting of three years of mainly theoretical training in a college, followed by one or two years of practical training at a government institute, were proposed. Convinced that the main demand was for a less specialised introduction to agricultural science, the commission made provisions for such courses to be taught in some of the intermediate colleges in the rural areas (Report IV : 109-110; V : 176-191; 339-340).

In addition to proposing a radical re-organisation of the college of Engineering in Bengal, and a substantial extension of its range of studies, they recommended the establishment of departments of technology in association with the university college of science to provide courses in subjects like technological chemistry, dyeing and tanning. But such courses in technology were not to be begun until adequate teaching facilities were assured, and the preliminary intermediate training properly established. Once started, the output of trained students was to be carefully controlled with the aid of advisory committees representing the various industries concerned (Report, V : 192-209; 340-342)[9]. Preparatory vocational courses were to be provided through the intermediate colleges, laying a firm foundation for future studies.

The commission endorsed the view that eventually high grade technical education must necessarily be reared on the foundations laid in the secondary schools (Report, III : 186). They further endorsed the complete separation of technical and industrial education and the provision for each at its own type of institution, i.e. at technical colleges of university rank for higher grade and at trade schools in industrial centres for the lower grade (Report, V : 149). The Civil Engineering Department of the Bengal Engineering College was found to be adequate by the commisision for turning out competent civil engineers of university rank. Consequently no fundamental changes in curriculum and instruction were made, though the provision for two years' practical training before the award of diplomas was recommended. Training of a lower grade in civil engineering to be given through technical schools was recommended for all engineering students at this level while special training in architecture was to be given for intending professional architects.

The commission was of the view that a university should play an increasingly important role in the development of training in commerce. However, they were wary of making provisions for degree courses in commerce on the ground that to do so would be premature. Instead they suggested the development of the study of commercial subjects within the existing honours courses in economics. It could be extended later when the training in the schools and intermediate colleges was sufficiently improved.

While advocating technological education as a corrective for a literary and bookish tradition, the commission sounded a caution : the former should not fail to be liberal in its outlook (Report V : 192). In sounding such a caution, the commission anticipates a much later principle, which was to have significant influence upon the curriculum and syllabus of technical education. The commission far outdated its own times in its plea for developing a "technical sense" in students which can be described as a combination of trained perception and a sense of judgement. It endorsed the view that a student of technology

> "--- needs a firm basis of accurate knowledge, a habit of mind, which is both scientific and practical, resourcefulness in grappling with difficulties and a quick appreciation of the element of cost in judging whether a new process is sufficiently matured for application upon a commercial scale".

(Report V : 196)

With its insistence on the training of the mind for flexibility, adaption and judgment, the commission was anticipating the concept of technician education that emerged in the late nineteen sixties.

Technical Education in the Pre-independence Era, 1919-1945 :

The Swadeshi Movement mentioned earlier led to two tangible consequences. One was the creation of a college of Engineering and Technology at Jadavpur in Bengal in 1907, which granted diplomas in engineering courses. Because of its association with the nationalist movement, it was not given official recognition and was kept out of the official system for a long time. The institution however, kept attracting students and many of them later went abroad to take British degrees in engineering, doing very well in these courses[10]. The other consequence was more diffuse but more pervasive : the creation of an awareness that education should be under Indian control, so that Indians might have a say in what was needed and what the content might be[11]. This pressure eventually led to the enactment of the Government Act of 1919, which established the system of diarchy in which education became a "transferred" subject and passed into the control of Indian ministers responsible to provincial legislature. This change gravely sabotaged the work of the Calcutta University Commission. Before the draft of a bill giving effect to the commission's proposals could be introduced, the transfer of responsibility for the University of Calcutta from the government of India to the government of Bengal took place. The latter was unable to undertake the reforms contemplated by the Commission due to financial stringency; and thereafter neither government did anything to implement the recommendations of the report (Richey 1923, I : 52; *Hundred years of the University of Calcutta*, 1957 : 195-197; 268-275).

Within the span of 25 years between 1919 to 1945 we find a gradual change in the concept of technical education in India, though in real terms there was no perceptible change except for the sharp increase in the number of institutions providing such education. Two documents on educational policy during this period, the Hartog (1929) and the Sargent (1944) reports[12], will be considered both for the actual recommendations that they offered and for the rationale which governed them. They sum up the British position on technical education in India in the pre-independence era.

Review of the Growth of Education in British India - Report of the Auxilliary Committee of the Indian Statutory Commission ["Hartog Report"] (1929) :

Precluded from making "a general survey of the whole field of Education in all its branches and aspects throughout British India" (Report : 2), the Committee was "primarily concerned with Education and its organisation in British India in relation to political and constitutional conditions and potentialities of progress (Ibid). Faced with the phenomenon of a representative government, education in India needed to make its functioning viable. For this purpose it was necessary to create a competent electorate as well as a body of trustworthy representatives and officials (Ibid : 3). The Committee saw the system of primary and higher primary schools as contributing to the former, while the system of secondary and higher education as producing the latter. Though they had to refer to the relationship between education and employment, the committee found that "it has been impossible" to "discuss in any detail" the questions of professional or technical education (Ibid : 5). Surveying the present scene, the committee found that the parents had no choice of the type of school to which they could send their children. Only one type was availabe[13], (Ibid : 104), through which a student would automatically come up to collegiate education. Among the measures suggested for remedying such lack of diversion, the committee recommended the retention of students at the middle vernacular schools for rural pursuits and the diversion of more boys to industrial and commercial courses at the end of the middle stage, both through a diversification of and options among courses (Ibid : 107). Another reason for over-crowding in general courses was identified as the government's policy in insisting on a university degree for its appointments. The committee suggested the introduction of special government examinations for appointments so that "the possession of a degree" could no longer be taken as "a higher qualification for service".

We include here some figures from the report to provide a picture of the state of technical education in India by 1927. The Calcutta University Commission had reported a four-tier hierarchy in the existing system of technical education, comprising of

A. University education, e.g. B. E. in civil engineering at Sibpur, a 4 year course followed by 1 year of practical training.

B. College Diploma courses, as in Sibpur, Dacca and Bankipur.

Usually a 3 years course, though some had an extra year of practical training thrown in.

C. Workshop Apprentice Courses, for which various independent arrangements existed.

D. Evening classes, usually lectures for people who were already on the job, at the level of apprentices.

The Hartog report shows the number of various types of institutions in existence in 1927. Fig. 2.2 below sets out the information in an adapted form.

Kinds of Institutions	Number in 1927
University Departments of Engineering	3
Engineering Colleges	4
Engineering Schools	10

Fig. 2.2 Showing the number of Engineering Institutions in India in 1927 (adapted from Table CXVII and CXVIII in Hartog : 393).

This information does not make clear which institution was imparting education at which stage of the hierarchy. For example, an engineering college could train at levels A, B and C, while an engineering school could train for levels B and C.

The Hartog report categorically stated that at the time vocational and industrial training had little contact with the educational system, and was therefore largely infructious (Report : 345). It was evident to the committee that attempts to introduce practical and vocational instruction in ordinary schools were unaccompanied by any clear aim of either such instruction or of its proper relationship to the ordinary school course (Ibid : 111). However, the sheer number of separate technical and industrial schools[14] had gone up considerably between 1917 and 1927, a matter of ten years, as table 2.3 below will testify.

Table 2.3
(From Hartog 1929, Table CXXVI : 397)

PROVINCES	No. of Technical & Industrial Schools		
	1917	1922	1927
Madras	40	41	63
Bombay	26	31	33
Bengal	59	86	153
United Provinces	28	37	111
Punjab	33	25	24
Burma	4	3	2
Bihar & Orissa	38	32	43
Central Provinces	9	7	2
Assam	7	12	15
Total for British India	251	276	450

Post-war Educational Development in India : Report by the Central Advisory Board of Education, January 1944 (Sargent Regport) :

In 1935, the Government of India enacted an Act, which divided all educational activities into two categories, as Central and Provincial subjects. The Central Advisory Board of Education (CABE) was revived in the same year and began examining critically one aspect of Indian education after another. The report of the Technical Education Committee was submitted in 1943, making substantial use of an earlier report by A. Abbott prepared in 1937, and drawing on the Spens report (1938) relating to Technical High Schools in Britain. The Sargent report incorporated the Technical Education Committee report in its overall plan for post-war educational development. The following references relate mainly to the Technical Education Committee report since it was used without any change in the Sargent report[15].

The sudden expansion of industry as a result of the war created a greatly increased demand for technicians of all grades, a demand which could not be satisfied by the earlier policy of importing technicians for the higher posts. So training facilities had to be provided locally. At the time the concept of technical education was changing in Britain and other countries[16], and needed to be redefined in the Indian context. The report proceeds to do this prior to offering its recommendations. The commisision took an overall view and as a result technical education was seen as an integral part of the general educational system. High school education was not to be a preliminary to University education, but a preparation for direct entry into occupations and professions (Sargent 1944 : 20). For this, the Commission proposed high schools of two types, the Academic and the Technical. At the middle level both would have a common core of "humanities" subjects, listed in the report. The medium of instruction recommended for all high schools was the mother tongue of the pupils, with English being taught as a compulsory second language.

Comments :

The Sargent report was the first comprehensive plan for national education in India. It was planning for a long term objective and was adjusted to post-war needs. A period of not less than forty years was considered the requisite period of time for bringing about the changes envisaged. It emphasised primary education since the present system did not provide "the foundation on which an effective structure could be erected" (Sargent 1944). The national system of education was inspired by the desire to provide equality of opportunity at every level of education. Technical education was specially emphasised, with the suggestion of provision for 75,000 places in technical institutions apart from the 25,000 places in the universities. However, before the schemes recommended could be implemented, British power was withdrawn from India on August 15, 1947. Hence, like the recommendations of the Calcutta University Commission, those made by the Sargent report were never applied to the Indian situation.

Notes :

1. The concept of society at the time was a fixed one, in which each had his ordained position. Education and behaviour patterns of a person had to be in keeping with his position in society. University education was the preserve of the upper classes. Practical skills were associated with science and were thought to be suitable training for the lower classes.

2. This has reference to the characteristic victorian view of life, which looked upon social order as a providentially arranged one, in which each person had a definite status according to birth or environment.

The higher classes merited a higher order of education, while useful and practical arts were reserved for the general run of the people.

3. The situation in Germany and France were very different.

4. This is supported by the Sadler Commission's criticism that the educated classes were unwilling to go in for technical education. Also, by 1882 the majority of the students in the Calcutta University chose to follow a literary or legal training.

5. Including what is now Orissa, Bangladesh and the North-Eastern States.

6. The first quinquennial report was written in 1886-87, for the period covering 1883-1887. They continued to be written for the years 1888-1892, 1893-97 and so on, till 1917-22.

7. In Serampore, a Dutch Colony in Bengal, a printing press was in existence in 1818, where Indian artisans did excellent work in devising the first face types in Bengali and several other Indian languages (Sur 1977 ; Bandopadhyaya 1979).

8. Radhakrishnan Commission mentions the date as 1842. Our date is taken from a contemporary report.

9. This anticipates the concept of manpower surveys in relation to industry and technical education.

10. Calcutta Doordarshan interview of Dr. Triguna Sen, former Union Minister for Edn, televised on 26.5.1980. Dr. Sen had also been associated with the Jadavpur University for a very long time.

11. Macaulay had rejected the idea of consulting Indians on education; Wood did not consider this necessary.

12. Fuller titles are : Review of the Growth of Education in British India. Report of the Auxilliary Committee of Indian Statutory Commission (1929); Post war Educational Development in India : Report by the Central Advisory Board of Education, January 1944.

13. This is a measure of success of Macaulay's advocacy of English

education and the choking of the growth of indigenous schools.

14. Presumably, these imparted C level courses, that is, workshop apprentice classes, though no clear cut indications are given.

15. Incidentally, John Sargent was also the Chairman of the Technical Education Committee.

16. The Spens Report (1938) in Britain was necessitated by such changes.

3

India's Post-Independence Policy on Technical Education

Post-Independence Policy : 1947-1973

Two events prior to 1947 and relating to technical education had consequences for post-independent India. The All India Council for Technical Education (AICTE) was created in 1945 and has been functioning till today, determining general policies and coordinating between various agencies. The N.A. Sarkar Committee set up in 1945 and reporting in 1946, dealt with the question of institutions of higher technological education in India. It was on the recommendations of this committee that the five Indian Institutes of Technology (IIT's) were set up in Bombay, Kharagpur, Kanpur, Madras and Delhi between 1951 and 1961. After independence, the University Education Commission 1948-49 (Radhakrishnan Commission), the Secondary Education Commission 1952 (Mudalier Commission) and the Education Commission 1964-66 (Kothari Commission) reviewed various aspects of education in India and made a number of recommendations for improving education in their respective reports. The main reason for appointing these commissions was the view that the entire basis of education in free India must be revolutionised (Nehru 1948). Based on these reports, a national policy in education was adopted in 1968. In relation to technical education, the Government of India Science Policy Resolution of 1958 is of immense importance. A related matter is the government's policy on language education. Since 1947, several man-power studies have also been undertaken to determine supply and demand of technical personnel.

The University Education Commission, 1948-49 (Radhakrishnan Commission) :

The University Education Commission explicitly relates education to life and the goals it is meant to achieve. These goals are social, political, economic as well as humane, commensurate with the status of India as a free and emerging nation. It is seen as being engaged "in a quest for democracy", realisable through the ideals of "justice, liberty, equality and fraternity" (Report : 36). The educational system, preparing the youth of the country for the future, "must find its guiding principle" in the very nature of the civilisation it hopes to build, and hence in "the aims of the social order for which it prepares" (Ibid : 36). It is aimed at the "realisation of the potentalities of each individual" fostering human dignity and social justice (Ibid : 37,36), and it must lead to the development of "a sense of perspective" (Ibid : 34), resulting in "intellectual vision, aesthetic judgement and practical power" (Ibid : 41). For such education subjects must be taught "as parts of a connected curriculum" (Ibid : 34). The total gamut of the content of teaching is then categorised under three heads as consisting of "our relation to things or nature", "our relation to men or society" and "our relation to values or the world of spirit" (Ibid : 39). Thus anyone who wishes to live intelligently in the modern world, should have some knowledge of selected materials from the three fields of science and technology, social studies and humanities (Ibid : 41). Thus the report stresses the unity of mind and the interdependence of knowledge.

It is within this general framework that the report's recommendations for technical and vocational education are to be seen. Dissatisfied that existing institutions were unable to provide the kind of education envisaged in the report, the commission recommended the setting up of institutions of a different kind (Ibid : 244, 247). The aim would be to produce "not merely men skilled in technology, but also sound, well-integrated individuals and citizens" (Ibid), capable of "a spirit of adventure, resourcefulness and self-reliance" (Ibid : 245). For achieving this, the report suggested the inclusion of courses in general education and of practical courses like business administration, labour relations and industrial finance within the technical curriculum (Ibid : 236). Works-training was to be an integral part of the course. The new institutions were to meet the emerging needs of the country (Ibid : 244).

The report stratified technical personnel according to the functions they performed :

(1) Senior Engineers and Administrators
(2) Engineering Scientists, Design and Development Engineers
(3) Engineers required for production, operation, maintenance and sale
(4) Technical Assistants and Designer Draftsmen
(5) Draftsmen, foremen and craftsmen (Ibid : 227-8),

and suggested an increase in the number of institutions catering to various grades, particularly for the training of grades 4 and 5 referred to above. The courses were to include courses in general education and in basic physical and engineering sciences. The first year or more of each course was to be common to all the branches of engineering (Ibid : 255). Larger number of fields and branches of engineering were to be covered.

Thus we see social, political and economic ideals dictating the curriculum, approach and subjects of technical education in Independent India.

The Education Commission : 1964-66 (Kothari Commission) :

Following the lead of the Radhakrishnan Commission, the Education Commission looked upon education as the main instrument of change for developing human resources, for realizing national aspirations and for meeting national challenges (Report : 1966). It had thus to be related to productivity and be used to hasten the processes of modernization (Ibid). In order to achieve these goals, priority must be given to the inclusion of science as a basic component of education, of work experience as a part of general education; to the vocationalisation of education to meet the needs of industry, agriculture and trade; and to the improvement of scientific and technical education and research at the university stage with special emphasis on agriculture and the allied sciences (Ibid). Science education had to be reinforced at all levels through the study of applications to local environments, thus necessitating changes in curricula and teaching (Ibid), the aim being to "promote understanding of basic principles", "develop problem-solving" as well as "analytical skills" and to promote the "spirit of enquiry and experimentation", so that a "scientific outlook" can become a part of life and culture (Ibid).

The report classifies technical training in terms of levels of skill and indicates the institutions responsible for such training :

(1) Research and design Engineers - with post graduate qualifications from the universities or IIT's
(2) Engineers - graduates trained in the regional and state colleges of engineering
(3) Technicians - diploma holders trained at polytechnic institutions[1]
(4) Semi skilled and skilled workers - trained at junior technical or in technical high schools (Ibid).

The commission made a number of recommendations, specially in connection with polytechnic education, relating to curricula and courses, equipment, teachers, location and industrial experience.

Science Education Policy in Post Independent India :

Post independent India followed a definitive policy on science education inspired mainly by the views of Pandit Jawaharlal Nehru, the first Prime Minister of free India, on science, science education and their relation to life. Convinced that it is only science which can "transform a economy of scarcity into one of abundance" (Nehru 1946 : 20-21), he had the country's economic plans formulated with the aim of expanding industrialization and the development of power resources to the utmost. For him,

> "The scientific approach are or should be, a way of life, a process of thinking, a method of acting and associating with our fellow men......"
>
> ***(Ibid : 624)***

This approach involves "the search for truth and new knowldege", "the refusal to accept anything without testing and trial", and the "capacity to change previous conclusions in the face of new evidence" (Ibid : 623, 624). The Scientific Policy Resolution of 1958 spell out how the transition is to take place :

> "The key to natural prosperity.....lies, in the modern agc , in thc cffcctivc contribution of three factors, technology, raw materials, and capital, of which the first is perhaps the most important, since the creation and adoption of new scientific techniques can, in fact, make up for a deficiency in natural resources and reduce the demand in capital. But technology can only grow out of the study of science and its application".
>
> ***(GOI, 1958)***

In order to be able to utilise the human materials for industrialisation, it is necessary to provide "education in science and training in technical skills" (Ibid). The aims of scientific policy is seen to be two-pronged. On the one hand, it must foster, promote and sustain the cultivation of science and scientific research; on the other it must encourage and initiate "programmes for the training of scientific and technical personnel", in order to fulfill the country's needs in science and education, agriculture and industry, and defence" (Ibid), the overall aim being to secure for the people of the country "all the benefits" that accrue from "the acquisition and application of scientific knowledge" (Ibid). Thus we see, inherent in the policy, a strong emphasis on technical education. Till now, however, the changes suggested were at the level of policy formulation only. The suggestions were taken up by the Working Group on Technical Education and Vocational Training, 1960 (hereafter referred to as TEVT report) so that the policy decisions could be translated into practice.

The Working Group on Technical Education and Vocational Training, 1960 :

The report made a survey of the types of institutions in existence providing technical education at various levels, tracing the development of polytechnics from senior vocational schools. It also mentions special institutions run by the Railways, Defence department and the Post and Telegraphs department. It identified polytechnics as those institutions which offered courses of three years' duration "in branches of immediate use to Government departments and industry" (Report, 1960). These were found all over the country, but the introduction of specialised courses was fairly recent. The report laid special emphasis on polytechnic education, suggesting that new thinking in regard to their objectives and functions was essential. They were to be organised in big cities and the number of courses was to be increased. These had to be established in appropriate relation to the country's social, educational and economic requirements. Technical and scientific changes might lead to a change in the nature of training, a fact that must be taken cognizance of in any programme for technical education, and there may be a case where one has to "rethink and reorganise methods of training as well as institutions" (Ibid : 22) Two concrete recommendations urged the setting up of manpower studies to be undertaken to specify the gap between need and availability of technically trained personnel and providing a larger margin for training rather than less.

Level of Technical Education :

From the various reports aleready mentioned, it has been seen that there have been attempts to categorise technical personnel in various ways. This was necessary because till the 1960's the technical education scene in India was rather chaotic. There was no uniformity of nomenclature either for the institutions imparting technical education or for their products. In order to bring about some uniformity in the use of termiology relating to various levels, and for distinguishing such levels unambiguously, the TEVT Report (1960) and the manpower surveys began using the terms "graduate engineers" and "diploma holders". At that time research and post-graduate qualifications in technical education was not available in India, so there was no term to refer to such a level. The Kothari Commission used the term "technician" for the first time to refer to diploma holders. In course of time, four distinct levels within technical education came to be distinguished. They were :

(i) Indian Institutes of Technology
(ii) Regional and State Colleges of Engineering
(iii) Polytechnics
(iv) Industrial Training Institutes

These are hierarchical in nature and provide different levels of training and skills. Table 3.1 below shows this :

Table 3.1
Showing Levels of Technical Education in India

Type of Institution	Entry Qualification	Category of Personnel	Qualification Given	Duration of course
IIT	Higher Secondary (+2) for Graduate course Degree for Post Graduate Course	Technologist	Graduate, Post Graduate and Research	5 yrs
Regional or State College of Engineering	Higher Secon- Secondary (+2)	Technical Personnel	Graduate Degree	4 yrs
Polytechnics	Secondary (10)	Technician	Diploma	3 yrs
Industrial Training Institute	Secondary (10)	Skilled Personnel	Certificate	1 yr

As can be seen from the above table, technologists hold post graduate and research degrees, technical personnel hold graduate degrees, technicians hold diplomas and skilled personnel hold certificates.

During the 1960's, as a direct fallout of the Science Education Policy and TEVT Report, the main thrust of Technical Education was on the

Diploma level, the most unplanned section within technical education. The reason was simple : in the changing scenario, the middle level technical personnel, the product of polytechnics, were considered to be the most crucial element for implementing the science policy of the country. The research and design technologists were expected to provide the theoretical base for technology, which the graduate engineers were to translate into reality. The middle level personnel were to be responsible for mediating between the skilled workmen and the degree holders. They were to be the bridge between the reality and the vision. For this reason their number had to be large. To implement this aspect of technical education, polytechnics were given a boost during the late sixties and early seventies. It was brought under a definitive plan so that the level of technical education could have uniformity not only across the country but also across the Commonwealth in matters of organisation, curricula and standard. In fact by 1973, polytechnic education became isomorphic within India, as the IIT's and engineering colleges already were. Because this is a newer development, it needs to be considered in some detail.

Education and Training of Technicians, Report of an Expert Conference, 1966 (Huddersfield Conference) :

At this juncture events taking place elsewhere had an impact on the planning and subsequent implementation of polytechnic education in India. The Commonwealth Education Liaision Committee organised an expert conference at the College of Education at Huddersfield, England, where representatives of various Commonwealth countries met, first to work out a definition of the scope and nature of technician education[2], and then to work out a workable curriculum and syllabus. The aim was to have a fairly equivalent standard of training for this group of technical personnel across the Commonwealth. When the Special Committee on the reorganisation and development of Polytechnic education in India submitted its report in 1971, it took into account the consensus reached at the Huddersfield conference and defined polytechnic education along the lines in tune with developments taking place elsewhere. By 1973, the new policy began to take effect.

Special Committee report on the reorganisation and development of Polytechnic education in India : 1970-71 (Damodaran Committee) :

The Damodaran Committee was set up following a suggestion by Prof. V.K.R.V. Rao, the then Union Minister for Education and Youth Services, made at the 20th meeting of the All India Council for Technical Education held on September 23, 1969, for examining the entire system of polytechnic education and for preparing a blue-print to reorganise all its aspects during the next ten years (Damodaran : 1). In order to carry these out, the committee undertook a sample survey and made a thorough analysis of the present system as to its adequacy vis-a-vis job requirements. In the process it defined clearly, for the first time, the scope and nature of technician education. This was necessary because, as the TEVT committee and the ManPower Group Survey (1963) had pointed out earlier, the scene for technical education presented a confused picture as to the nomenclature of institutions, the designation of employees within industry, and the functions carried out by technical personnel. There was a constant overlap of labels, categories, qualifications and functions. The TEVT Committee as well as the Manpower Supply had adopted the practice of using the terms "graduate engineers" and "diploma holders" to distinguish the qualifications irrespective of the kinds of institutions where these were obtained. The designations in industry were no help either. A Chargeman or a Foreman could be either a graduate engineer or a diploma holder. Often, the functions a graduate engineer and a diploma holder had to perform were identical. The report not only spelt out the nature of technician education, but also specified by name the kind of institutions associated with diploma level technical training. Hence, a clear cut definition of "polytechnic institutions" may be said to date from 1971. Moreover, a national policy on technician education and the new curricula in keeping with the clearly defined concept of "technician education" became operative across the country during 1973[3].

The national policy for polytechnics adopted on the basis of the recommendations of the Damodaran Committee resulted in the isomorphism of such institutions. Hence it is necessary to consider in some detail the findings and recommendations of the report.

Reviewing the development of technician education in India, the report finds very little growth or development taking place before independence (Damodaran : 5). This is not surprising since the growth of technical education depends on "the socio-economic and industrial conditions of the country" and its development is controlled by the "needs and requirements of the economy" (Ibid). But since independence there has been a rapid expansion in the number of institutions ; whereas there were 53 diploma level institutions in existence in 1947, in 1966 there were 284 (Ibid : 5). This was due to the changed circumstances in the country, and hence it was vital to the economy and development of the country that its technician education be of the right kind.

The report quotes the definition of the term "technician" adopted by the I.L.O. and that adopted at the 12th Session of the General Conference of UNESCO in 1962 to give an idea of the nature of the knowledge and functions expected of such a person. It further refers to the definition of a "technician" arrived at by the Huddersfield Conference as people employed in the broad spectrum of occupations lying between the craftsman on the one hand and the professional or technologist on the other. Based on these, the report evolved its own definition of a technician as a middle level employee, functioning between the craftsman and the technologist, and required to show applications of technical knowledge higher than that of the former but below that of the latter and possessing proficiency in skills higher than that of a technologist but lower than that of a skilled worker (Ibid : 9). The report also lists a number of functions related to engineering industries which a technician needs to perform. In fact the report finds technicians distributed in three broad areas in terms of functions : design and production; laboratory testing and analysis; and sales, stores and costing, the greatest proportion being involved in design and production (Ibid : 12).

The report then proceeds to analyse the kind of abilities technicians need, as a preliminary to the reorganisation of polytechnic education in terms of curricula and teaching methods. A technician is concerned with the work of others : collaboration with the engineer and supervision of the work of the craftsmen is an essential part of his job. Hence he needs to have an awareness of the nature of the task and its associated problems at both these levels. A broad basic training is thus essential for him (Ibid : 10). The main qualities needed for him include knowledge of the basic technology in the chosen field, a knowledge of engineering practical situations and personnel qualities and leadership ability (Ibid : 13). In all fields a technician requires the ability to communicate with his colleagues at senior and junior levels, through reports, instructions and so on, and hence needs fluency in the use of the written and the spoken word. Hence polytechnic curriculum cannot be geared to a narrow specialisation, as some of the abilities mentioned above are best built on the basis of sound general education (Ibid : 10). The main objective of technician education programme of polytechnics is then to give the student a sound broad based knowledge of a chosen field, supplemented by actual practical experience in industry, business or commerce, as the case may be. In order to face the ever increasing rate of technological change and scientific progress, the technician has to be adaptable, flexible and must have a broad outlook, thus calling for broad-based courses including liberal and humanistic studies (Ibid : 11).

Notes :

1. The label polytechnic is used for the first time to refer to a particular type of institution imparting technical education. This was possible in view of the survey carried out by the Working Group on Technical Education and Vocational Training, 1960. This level was considered to be of crucial importance for the development of the country.

2. These are nongraduate middle level technical personnel holding diplomas and corresponding to grade 3 mentioned in the Kothari Commission.

3. Personal communication.

4

Science Education and Technical Education

Since technical studies consist of the applied aspects of the findings of science, the history of technical education cannot be separated from that of science education. In the Introduction the three major goals of science have been considered and it has been shown how these interact with societal changes to influence technical education (Figs 1.1 and 1.2). In this chapter we will consider how policy makers in post-independent India have perceived the relationship between science education and technical education.

Relationship of Technical Education to Science Education :

It is outside the scope of the present book to delve into the philosophy of science education and how it relates to technical education and its philosophy. However, it is necessary to consider how education policy makers in post-independent India viewed the matter. The Radhakrishnan Commission, considering the content of teaching, found one category to be man's relations to things or nature (Report : 39). According to the commission, the desire to understand nature gives us science, whereas the desire to "use knowledge of nature for definite ends" gives us technology (Ibid). In fact, the principles of science are seen to be so closely related to technology, that a knowledge of these is considered to be essential for any technical course. The guidelines for curriculum planning for technical education at all levels reflect this view. As the Scientific Policy Resolution stated it "-----technology can only grow out of the study of science and its applications."

Hence it is relevant to refer to the text of the Science Policy Resolution of 1958 in some detail. According to this document,

> "The key to national prosperity lies, ... in the modern age, in the effective combination of three factors, technology, raw materials, and capital, of which the first is perhaps the most important, since the creation and adoption of new scientific techniques can, infact,

> make up for a deficiency in natural resources and reduce the demand on capital. But technology can only grow out of the study of science and its applications".
>
> ***(SPR : 1958)***

The document further points out that "the use of human material for industrialisation demands its education in science and training in technical skills". The Resolution, following this perspective, comes to the following conclusion :

> "The development of science at an ever increasing pace has led to the widening of the gap between the advanced and the backward countries more and more. Hence the aims of India's scientific policy will be
>
> (i) to foster, promote and sustain the cultivation of science and scientific research
>
> (ii) to ensure adequate supply of research scientists
>
> (iii) to encourage and initiate, with all possible speed, programmes for the training of scientific and technical personnel, on a scale adequate to fulfil the country's needs in science and education, agriculture and industry; and defence
>
> (iv) and, in general, to secure for the people of the country all the benefits that can accrue from the acquisition and application of scientific knowledge".
>
> ***(Ibid)***

The shape and content of technical education in India then has been shaped by the scientific policy of the nation. This can be seen reflected in the curriculum proposed by the Damodaran Committee and set out in Fig. 4.1.

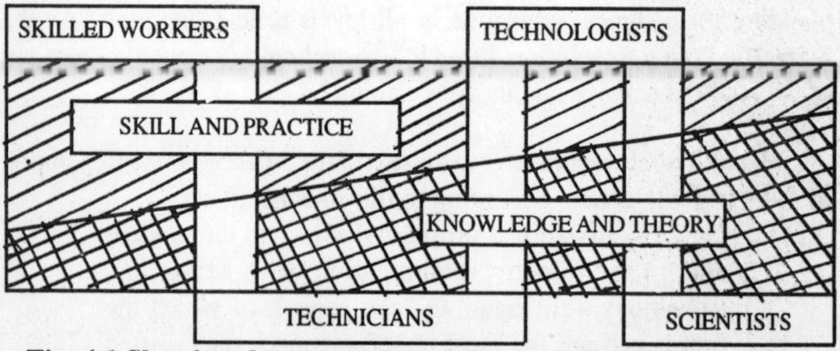

Fig. 4.1 Showing the proportion of theory and practice required for various levels of technical personnel (from Damodaran : 11)

Objectives of Technical Education :

According to the Radhakrishnan Commission, education has to be flexible, capable of adaptation to the changing needs and conditions of man (Report : 44). If this is true of education in general, then it is even more true of technical and technician education. A UNESCO Report (1978)[1] reviewing the policy and planning of technical and vocational education in 23 countries including India, found a consensus existing as to the two major policy goals for such education. These goals, in accordance with the Revised Recommendations adopted by the General Conference of UNESCO at its eighteenth session in 1974, are :

(a) Technical and vocational education should be geared to fulfilling the man-power requirements for economic development and the social requirements for employment.

(b) Technical and vocational education should be developed in such a way as to provide broader educational opportunities for an increasing proportion of the population.

(Report : 38)

In India then, the process of technical and vocational education is expected to contribute to the achievement of society's goals of greater democratization and social, cultural and economic development, while at the same time developing the potential of individuals for active participation in the establishment and implementation of these goals. It is further expected to lead to an understanding of the scientific and technological aspects of contemporary civilization in such a way that men comprehend their environment and are capable of acting upon it while taking a critical view of the social, political and environmental implications of scientific and technological change. Technical and vocational education thus should be firmly rooted in a broad-based general education. Technician or polytechnic education, as the middle level of technical education, shares all of the foregoing objectives along with its other levels.

According to the Damodaran Committee Report (1971), the main objective of technician education programmes in polytechnics is to give the student a sound broad based knowledge of a chosen field combined with actual experience in industry or business or commerce, as the case might be. A technician must have a broad band of abilities : he must have a mastery of techniques relevant to immediate employment and an understanding of science and mathematics which is firm enough to permit further extention to new applications and situations (p. 10). In the area of human and social aspect, technician education must lead to a development of confidence and a competence for self-employment (Ibid, para 7). In other words, technician courses, being broad based, must have provisions for diversification : preparing a student for entrance into a technician function, facilitating mobility as well as future occupational advancement (Ibid, paras 15, 16). Polytechnic education should aim to develop practical skills and an attitude to understand, appreciate and apply concepts to practical situations (Ibid, para 37). The main qualities expected of diploma holders irrespective of the nature of the process or the organisations involved, are the following, according to the Report :

(a) a knowledge of the basic technology in the chosen field,

(b) a knowledge of engineering practice in industry,

(c) an ability to apply technical knowledge to practical situations,

(d) personnel qualities and leadership ability.

(Ibid : 13)

The draft Science and Technology Plan 1974-79 (1973) identifies its immediate concerns as being the questions of "how to harness science" for the "improvement in the quality of life of the common man", in the process reaching "higher levels of productivity", achieving "efficient utilisation of wastes", and in general, inculcating "an atmosphere of efficiency" and assembling the elements of a "progressive excellence in technology".

Content of Curriculum and Methodology :

It is not enough to set objectives and goals, no matter how well specified. Unless these can be implemented, setting up of goals becomes an exercise in futility. Policy formulations indicate the objectives and the nature of the desired "product". To arrive at this point, there must be an interface between policy and product, embodying measures, steps and processes which may bring about the transition from objectives to the product. The content of the curriculum, syllabus design and appropriate methodology are instruments of such transition. However, the translation of goals into a curriculum is neither a direct nor an easy and simple task. In a lead paper at the Huddersfield Conference, Chandrakant dwelt at length on the problem :

> "The development of a curriculum for technician training is not a mere academic expercise. It takes in a number of important practical aspects like the present status of technology in a country and its future needs, the precise functions of a technician within the overall social and economic structure of industry, the pattern of man-power employment in each type of industry and relationship between engineers, technicians and skilled workers, the level of technical professional competences demanded of them and the position of technical education within the country's educational system."
>
> ***(Chandrakant 1967 : 36)***

The curriculum thus, is a crucial stage in technician education, its quality determining the success or otherwise of the objectives set up by a national policy. In India, the innovations in the new policy concern both the content and methodology of technician education.

The Damodaran Committee conceives of the curriculum as being based on a clear definition of objectives, first, the "specific" ones of "technician specialities" and second, the "general" ones of technician education (Report, para 28). Spelt out in detail, a curriculum of this kind may be seen to have at least the following five components :

(i) technical education (theory)
(ii) technical education (practical)
(iii) technology (theory)
(iv) technology (practical)
(v) general education.

Theoretical technical education refers to that general background of mathematics, physics, chemistry, engineering drawing etc. which constitute the theory upon which depends a proper understanding of the techniques of which the technician must acquire a mastery. This technical basis should also be sufficient to enable the technician to cope with developments which might arise in his field after he has qualified. The practical technical education refers to the laboratory and experimental work which is concomitant with the theory. The technological theory refers to theory relevant to the actual equipment with which the technician is concerned and to the specific techniques which he has to exercise. Practical technology is concerned with the acquisition of the necessary skills which the technician needs for doing his job. This may well include basic manual skills similar to those possessed by the corresponding craftsmen. His theory is to serve as a background to enable him to do the practical work well and with certainty and expertise. The general educational component should include liberal elements such as communication, humanities and social studies, history of science and technology, civics, physical education, industrial organisation, human relations, materials and management, concepts of system engineering, industrial safety, economics, law, music, art, drama and languages. An important aim of this component should be to imbue the student with a clear concept of the importance of the job for which he is training, and help him acquire an understanding of the social context in which he lives and of the processes of social change. Entrepreneurial skills and communicational skills appropriate to the technician's job and his role in society are also to be developed through this component, so that an appreciation of the social and economic implications of science, technology, industrial and commercial activities may develop.

Achieving the right mix of the components is the significant initial step for the curriculum. The second step is concerned with syllabus making, specifying the topics within a particular area, indicating the depth of treatment for these, incorporating the principles of latest theoretical knowledge in the field, identifying the methodology inherent in such knowledge and ensuring the instruction of the kind which promotes the development and growth of the individual intellectually and emotionally. Above all there should be flexibility built in within the curriculum to allow for adaptations and modifications as the need arises.

Such new objectives and new orientations cannot be developed through the time-honoured practice of using descriptive lectures in the classroom and set exercises in the laboratories and workshops. In order to develop practical skills involving application of principles, project work and workshop practice are necessary. These are to be based on real problems involving industrial and commercial practice and procedures. The main criteria in planning laboratory and practical work should be to see whether these (a) further a clear inderstanding of the scientific principles taught ; (b) foster innovation and original thinking ; (c) help develop an ability in the creative use of knowledge and an ability for critical appraisal of test results ; (d) develop an appreciation of and the facility in the use of the experimental, and the approach to problem solving ; and (e) encourage fabrication and assembly of simple types of instruments and scientific apparatus (Damodaran 1971, paras 40-45), Apart from text books, additional and alternative teaching tools like programmed instruction and audio-visual aids need to be used. In order to develop mental skills or the ability in the application and creative use of knowledge and to foster independent thinking, tutorials, problem solving sessions, project work, seminars and case studies have to be used. The teaching has to be problem-centred rather than concept centred, as it is today. Specially the teaching of languages, mathematics and physical sciences will be effected, since the teaching of these subjects will have to be application based. Innovation is also necessary for the rapid transmission of a vast amount of knowledge, made essential by the current explosion of knowledge, making traditional modes inefficient.

Methodology is further related to the way a technician course is organised : whether it is a full-time pre-employment corse, a full time in-service course, a sandwich course or a block-release course. The allocation of time, the relationship of the components of the curriculum to each other, and the sequence of the components will, each in its turn, influence the methodology.

Whatever has so far been said about technician education, in equally applicable to other levels of technical education.

Notes :

1. Developments in Technical and Vocational Education : A Comparative Study. Paris, 1978.

5

The Role of English in Technical Education

It is customary to look upon technical education as consisting of skills for practical application and theories underlying such applications. In chapter four we have seen the varying proportions of these two aspects at various levels of technical education. However, it is not at all customary to focus on the role and importance of language in technical education. The present chapter is an attempt to ascertain the place of language in technical education, first by reviewing the role of language as envisaged by the various policy decisions, and secondly, by examining, in some detail, the demands made on language by technical education.

Policy Decisions on the Use of Language for Technical Education

In this context it is relevant to consider what "technical education" means. The report of the Technical Education Committee (1943), which formed part of the Sargent Report (1944), defined technical education in the Indian context. According to this report, technical education is not "merely a special training for industrial employment" but must "form a link between education and industry". Technical instruction, thus being wider and more liberal than it had been in the past, must include the scientific principles underlying the processes of manufacture, as well as the processes themselves, while linking up the sciences of production and business organisation with the arts of design and salesmanship. Thus technical education was viewed as a broad-based discipline providing for personal growth as well the ability to take part in the economic growth of the country.

As we have already seen in chapter three, the post-independent policies on education emanated from a definite philosophy of education related to the social and economic development of an independent nation. This had significant implications for curriculum and methodology at every level of technical education. As a result, the IIT's, engineering colleges and polytechnics included humanities subjects in their curriculum (cf Chapter 4).

For instance, it was proposed (Damodaran) that technician curriculum should comprise "an integrated group of subjects of study", arranged in proper sequence and leading to "the general objectives of technician education" and to "the specific objectives of technician specialities" (Ibid : 20). It should also lay the academic foundation for students aspiring to higher qualifications. Following those principles, a framework showing relative proportion of various components was drawn up in the Damodaran Committee report, shown below in Table. 5.1.

Table 5.1
Showing an Integrated Curricula for Polytechnics
(adapted from Damodaran : 20,21)

	Groups of subjects to be studied	%
(a)	General Studies, including language, management subjects, industrial safety, labour laws and so on	10%
(b)	Basic and applied sciences and mathematics	15% - 20%
(c)	Technical Studies : (i) Principles (Theory) (ii) Basic Speciality (electives)	20% - 30%
(d)	Practice (i) Design/Drawing (ii) Technical Laboratory or Workshop (iii) Project and Field Work	40% - 50%

The draft plan for Science and Technology, 1974-79, published in 1973, specifically states that such a plan is to be used as an instrument for the attainment of national goals :

> "--- while deriving its imperatives from the developmental and security goals which the nation sets for itself, the plan must also ensure that the opportunities which science and technology can provide will also help shape those very goals...... [It is] a plan to harness, science and technology for achieving the goals and programmes of the fifth plan. Consequently, even the direction of basic research and the man-power training effort that is often clearly

> associated with it, will need to be influenced by socio-economic goals".
>
> ***(Draft plan 1973)***

In fact the priority seems to be the development of the individual in order to achieve economic and social goals. This is in direct contrast to pre-independence policy when a knowledge of facts and skills was considered adequate. However, this priority does not preclude knowledge, but looks upon knowledge as an instrument for achieving societal goals. Hence the methods of science must also be in tune with this. A consequence of viewing technical education from this perspective is that it is seen as a continuing process throughout an individual's life time, and not as a terminal event in one's youth. This involves, above all, a change in attitude towards education, viewing it as a life-long process which should

> --- aim less at training young people to practice a given trade or profession than at equipping them to *adapt themselves* to a variety of jobs, at *developing their capacities* continuously, in order to keep pace with developing production methods and working conditions. It should help to achieve *optimum mobility in employment* and facilitate *conversion* from one profession or branch of a profession to another".
>
> (emphasis in the original)
>
> ***(Asher : Learning To Be 1974 : 196)***

In this context, we shall first consider the various policy recommendations made in relation to the language to be used as the medium of instruction for technical education. Secondly, we will consider the implications of such recommendations.

The University Education Commission went into the question of the language to be adopted as the medium of instruction in great detail and arrived at a position which can at best be described as ambivalent. On the one hand it recommends that for the majority, higher education should be "through the instrumentality of their regional language" (Radhakrishnan : 323), since regional languages were to be the principal media of instruction at all stages (Ibid); on the other, though it emphatically declares that in independent India English "cannot continue to occupy the place of state language as in the past", (Ibid : 316), and that ultimately "English will disappear from the scene" (Ibid : 325), it also equally emphatically avows that English "must continue to be studied" (Ibid). Similar juxtapositions occur repeatedly : English is to be replaced by the federal language Hindi in the universities (Ibid : 322, 324, 326), but no university student should be allowed to take a degree "unless he acquires the ability to read English fluently and with comprehension" (Ibid : 325).

The report did not mention specifically the medium of instruction in technician education, but the general drift of the recommendations suggest that at this level English was already being used and that it ought to be replaced by an Indian language, federal or regional. It did take up the problem of scientific and technological terminology, and recommended the adoption of international terms, with appropriate Indianization of pronunciation and spelling. It had no clear out recommendation for what it termed "quasi-technical terms" (Ibid : 315), that is, terms which have other uses beside the strictly technical one. Apart from terminology, no other problem related to the use of a language as the medium of instruction was dealt with[1]. The Kothari Commission (1966) however, specified quite unequivocally that the medium of instruction in the polytechnics has to be English. For IIT's and engineering colleges, the medium of instruction was English and there was no controversy at this level.

The Huddersfield Conference held in 1966, acknowledged the fact that in many commonwealth countries (including India), technician education was imparted through English, and for this reason English was included in the proposed course content (Report : 65). One of the areas identified by the report, where the technician needed great competence, was that of communication, both in speech and writing (Ibid : 62), for functioning on the job, as well as for receiving education through language. Some of the actions technicians need to perform are diagnosing faults, report writing, giving clear instructions, understanding instructions, supervising and so on. Hence the report emphasised the dual nature of English "as a technical subject" and as "communication skill" (Ibid : 90).

The Damodaran Committee unequivocally asserts that the study of the English language should not only be emphasised but also developed as a tool of effective communication for technical purposes (Report, para 35). It envisages language study as an essential component of general education, aiming at the development of communication skills and personal attitudes and qualities (Ibid : 20). Though it does not specifically mention that this language should be English, yet it is quite clear that English is indicated. However, the report does not take up the question of the medium of instruction at all and it is difficult to speculate what the report might have thought on this matter. In the event the state directorates of technical education decided whether English or some other Indian language was to be used as the medium of instruction. However, for IIT's and Engineering colleges English is considered to be the language for developing communication skills.

Language as a medium of instruction :

When a language is used as a medium of instruction, certain demands are made on it. It becomes a vehicle or a tool for carrying and conveying whatever the aims of education might be. Some of these are providing information, organisation of ideas, events and facts and also the way education has to be managed. The students must have a certain degree of competence in the language to be able to do these things. When the language concerned is the mother tongue of the students, the problem is not so acute. But when it is one other than the mother tongue, then two factors become absolutely crucial. One is the attainment of a minimum competence or the threshold level of the language concerned; the other is the way in which the language is applied for the functions of education. A lack in the former means that the student is unable to comprehend what is going on in the classroom. For example, the student may not understand what the teacher is saying. An incompetence in the latter means that the student is unable to proceed beyond rote memorization or restatement of principles and laws towards application and extrapolation[2]. Hence if a language which is not the mother tongue of the student, is to be used as the medium of instruction, then it must be ensured that first, a minimum level of competence in the language has been reached; and second, the uses of the language which are necessary, must be used in the way intended. A minimum level of competence does not, necessarily or automatically, lead to the deployment of the language for a particular purpose. If English has to be used as a medium of instruction for technical education, these prerequisites have to be ensured and then the actual uses have to be developed through the curriculum.

If we look a little more closely at the demands made on a language used as the medium of instruction, we find that it has to perform certain tasks like explaining, describing, defining, glossing or parapharsing, organising information and imposing a structure on it, relating it to existing knowledge of various kinds (e.g. social, cultural, educational, technical), reasoning out conclusions and solutions, presenting arguments for and against by weighing evidence, and relating to non-verbal information as well as to various tasks relevant for class managment. Moreover, apart from the information conveyed, the structure and nature of the subject as well as of the discipline, must be conveyed through instruction. These may not have overt formulations, but the way the subject is handled may indicate these. For example, precision and explicitness associated with a technical subject can be conveyed through the language used. But such qualities, contrary to popular belief, are not inherent to any particular language, but develop when there is a need for it. The case of English can be taken as a clear example. Francis Bacon, who inspired the advancement of science in the modern world through an elaborate study of scientific methodology and attempted to work out the whole scheme of what the body of science could be, initially wrote in Latin. However, it was mainly due to his inspiration and efforts that English began to be used for scientific purposes, including its use in the work of the Royal Society[3]. However, once such features become part of the use of a language in a particular domain, then those features define that particular use. English as the language of instruction and English as related to a particular subject are associated with a number of features which go beyond the simple question of technical terminology or quasi technical vocabulary. That these features are neither easily definable nor uniquely associated with a particular domain, is not an argument which invalidates the observation.

English as a subject :

The University Education Commission was convinced that though English will eventually cease to be used as the medium of instruction, it must still continue to be studied, as a means of preventing our isolation from the world and "the living stream of evergrowing knowledge" (Radhakrishnan : 325). A knowledge of English is essential for access to knowledge and the acquisition of "the ability to read with falicity (sic)" is essential for going on to higher education. The plea is clearly for the study of English as a subject. The Damodaran Committee's recommendation of the study of the English language being emphasised as a tool of effective communication (Report, para 35) has generally been understood to indicate the study of English as a subject[4].

The objectives set up by the University Education Commission were access to knowledge and hence the ability to read with understanding.

The Damodaran Committee's objectives appear to be more comprehensive : effective communication for technical purposes. This will include both written and spoken communication of various kinds, and cover a wide range of abilities. These may relate primarily to the job situation but cannot totally neglect the study situation. The syllabus for English as a subject in the polytechnics then must be geared to the development of a wide range of skills and abilities in language, needed in the study situation as well as in the job situation.

In the IIT's effective communication for technical purposes is assumed to be part of the learner's ability. This assumption is nowhere stated explicitly, nor is it spelt out what such an assumption entails. It is implied in what is included in the syllabus. The humanities component includes among other subjects, literature in English, the aim being the refinement of sensibilities. In colleges of Engineering too, the syllabus is literature based and does not address itself explicitly to the skills of communication. In the polytechnics, some attempts have been made to develop skills of communication through English.

The Relationship between Technical Curriculum and Language Syllabuses :

The University Education Commission's report testifies to the fact that in post independence India the objectives for learning English has changed. It stands to reason that the kind of syllabus which had been current till that time should be found to be inappropriate for achieving the changed objectives. This kind of syllabus, mainly consisting of literary pieces of various genres, had been intended for imbibing a "liberal education", through which the mind could be trained, sensibilities sharpened, and reason as well as the intellect honed. Imparting various skills in the use of language, leading to effective communication, clearly calls for a syllabus whose content and methodology is distinct from those of a literature syllabus.

For instance, let us take the case of polytechnics. If English is the medium of instruction in polytechnics, the students are immediately faced with two problems. One is the change in the medium of instruction, from the regional language in the schools to English in the polytechnic. School courses in English can hardly be described as preparatory ones. Receiving education through English is novel and confusing for the majority of the polytechnic students who come from regional language schools. The second problem relates to the mode of instruction : the lecture. Receiving education through lectures in English means being able to listen to and understand continuous spoken English. This spoken discourse is not "controlled" in any way by means of vocabulary, syntax, organisation and speed. If lectures are watered-down versions of text-book discourse, then the syntax is likely to be complex, the lexis (excluding special terminology) is likely to be outside the repertoire of the student[5], and the speed of normal delivery too fast for them. As far as I am aware, no research has been done in the Indian situation as to how much information and comprehension from a lecture given in English filters down to the students. But it is not difficult to see why polytechnic students are likely to have problems in following lectures given in English. Lectures are generally intended to provide new information and an understanding of new concepts. This is not likely to take place if the lectures are incomprehensible. For students of IIT's and regional engineering colleges, understanding lectures in English is not likely to be problematic, though some students of state engineering colleges may facc problems.

Another source of information, apart from lectures, is books - text and reference books. Students must be able to read well enough to extract the necessary information from written discourse in English, which uses verbal means as well as non-verbal ones in the form of charts, tables, figures, graphs, formulaes, diagrams and the like. They must also be able to display their knowledge and understanding through written discourse. Hence, for the purposes of their study within the polytechnic, students must be able to handle English in certain ways. These ways are related to their courses in technical subjects as well as to those in science and humanities. The content of such courses is subject specific but is embodied through English. The question needs to be asked, as to how a course in English would be related to these uses. What its content would be, and what methodology it should utilise, thus assume immense significance.

If English is not the medium of instruction, then how should the course in English be related to the rest of the curriculum ? Listening to lectures and writing assignments and examinations through English are no longer required, but the reading of books written in English cannot be entirely done away with, though the proportion may be reduced. For both groups the requirements for communicating in English on the job remains. Another need that is not blatantly obvious is that of being able to perform well in interviews held through English - which relates to

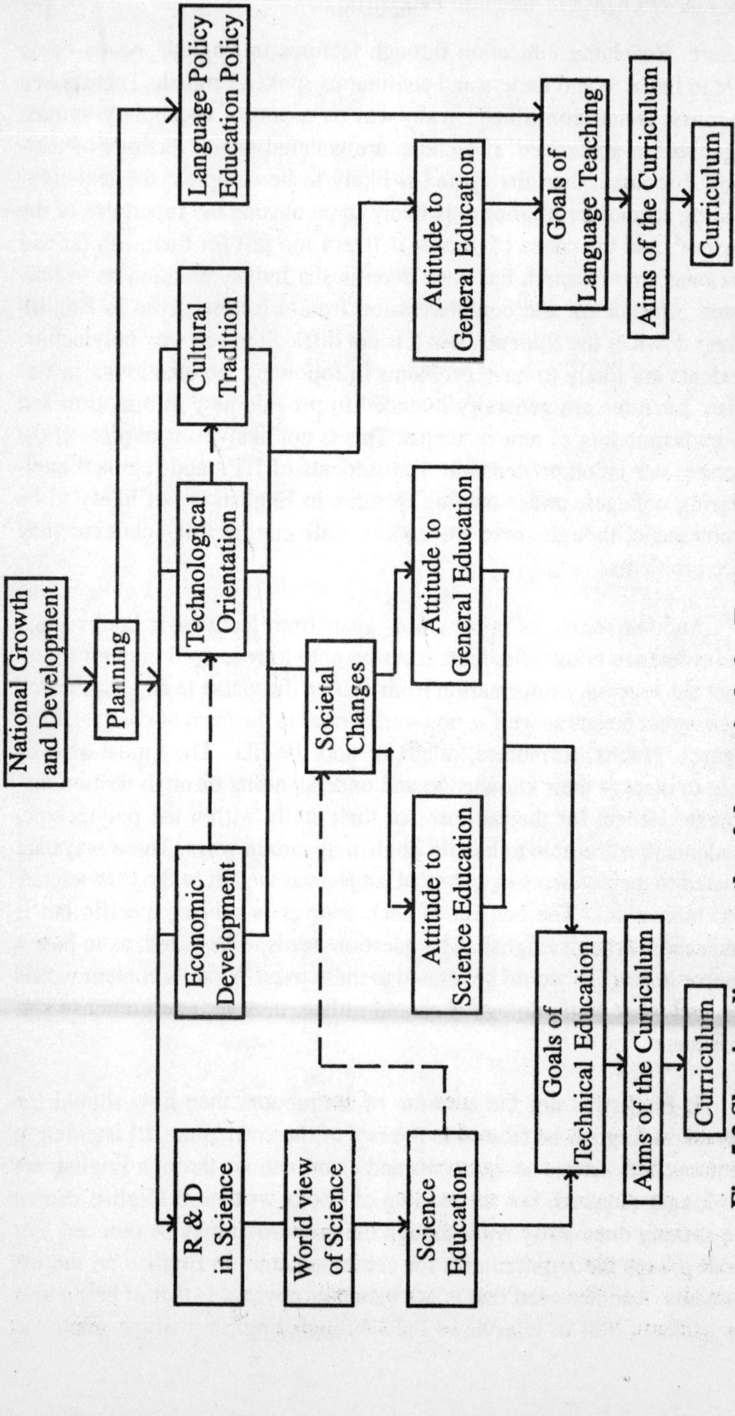

Fig. 5.2 Showing diverse paths of the curricula for Technical Education and Language Teaching

spoken exchanges.

The basic issue for a language syllabus then relates to the question of whether it can cater to the needs generated by the rest of the curriculum or whether it caters to those generated by itself. Fig. 5.2 sets out the problems.

In order to draw up a language course which is relevant to technical education, it is not enough to consider the goals generated by language education and whatever else it may entail; the needs of technical education are also to be taken into consideration. Fig. 5.2 illustrates how these two sets of goals can take diverse paths. In order to make the language syllabus for technical education relevant and viable, it is necessary to find a principled way of relating the two sets of goals, assigning priorities and determining the weight of the various factors. Fig. 5.3 below shows a possible relating of the two sets of goals, where the goals of language teaching are subordinated to the goals of technical education to produce aims of the curriculum which are consonant with those of technical education. The Damodaran Committee in fact, had taken this path.

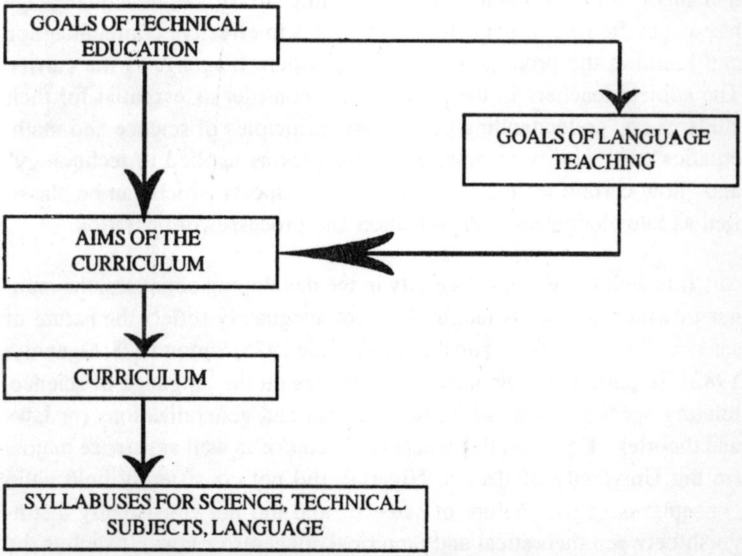

Fig. 5.3 Showing adjustment of various goals for technical education (only relevant components shown)

Under such an adjustment, many of the goals of language education as such may be undermined. The selection, emphasis and relative prominence given to goals are likely to be somewhat different from those for language education in general.

What, then, are the language needs of technical students ? If we consider the use of a language in terms of the four skills of listening, speaking, reading and writing, such needs can be characterised in the following manner.

First of all, learners need to attend to lectures given in English on technical and science subjects. This means the passing on of concepts and the structure of the discipline through language.

Instruction :

To understand how these work, it is necessary to consider various aspects of instruction for science and technology through a second language and related research, drawing inferences for technical education. For convenience the example of a polytechnic will be used to illustrate the point. The aim of instruction in the polytechnic is to impart the knowledge, attitudes and abilities which will make the student a "good" technician. For educators and policy planners, this involves viewing technician education as one for "life", a learning "to BE", in which language has a specific role to play. This role relates to effective communication and learning the processes of learning, where language is the carrier. The subject teachers in the polytechnics consider as essential for their students an "understanding of the basic principles of science and mathematics", an "ability to grasp the principles as applied to technology" and "how certain technologies worked", - aspects which can be classified as knowledge and its application and processes of operation.

It is well known that specially in the developing countries, the manner in which science is taught does not adequately reflect the nature of science (Weaver 1964; Abubaker 1969; Cole 1975; Simon 1978; Ogunniyi 1982). In particular, Ogunniyi concentrates on the language of science, relating specifically to scientific concepts and generalizations (or laws and theories). He found that teachers of science as well as science majors (in the University of Ibadan, Nigeria), did not consistently hold valid conceptions of the "nature of science" and did not consistently distinguish between theoretical and empirical concepts or laws. If such is the case, then technician education, which depends upon the application of the principles of science, will not be conceived of in its true nature.

In the Indian situation as well, the manner of instruction is likely to obscure the nature of science and technician education. In the polytechnic, the applications of the basic principles of science and mathematics are considered, while the principles themselves are usually assumed to have been acquired in school. In actual practice, this cannot be taken for granted. In a study concerning the knowledge of physics and chemistry of engineering students, Simon (1978) found that students are, in many ways, "false beginners" to advanced scientific thinking. Straightforward covering of materials in school often results in knowledge remaining half-digested, leading to memorisation. Simon suggests that the development of concepts, a time consuming process, requires novel teaching techniques, unusual questions to excite interest and test understanding, and bombarding with a variety of examples on the same theme, providing elaboration and making memorisation near impossible. That various teaching strategies may increase or decrease students' science achivement and attitude towards science is generally accepted (Mallinson 1947; Rosen 1956; Pella 1961; Glass 1967; Bradley 1968; Pella and Sherman 1969; Yager, Eugen and Snider 1969, Connel 1971; Tamir 1976; Mayfield 1976; Bates 1978; Case 1980; Harty and Al-Faleh 1983; Hewson and Hewson 1983). The laboratory small group experimentation method is one type of instruction which may facilitate the development of process skills and the spirit of enquiry and orient the students towards the realistic role of scientists (Yager, Eugen and Snider 1969; Pella 1969; Fisher 1973).

In schools in India, science is taught traditionally, through a straightforward covering of knowledge, so that when students come to the polytechnic, their knowledge of scientific laws and principles is not readily amenable to application. The implication is that the teaching in the polytechnic will have to be of a different kind if the skills of application and extrapolation, flexibility and adaptability are to be developed in the learners.

So far we have considered the matter of learning the principles of science in relation to the techniques used for teaching[6], irrespective of the language through which teaching is imparted. We will now look at the relationship between the language of instruction and achievements in science. In general, scientific technical personnel and teachers hold the view that language is no barrier to the comprehension of technical subjects[7]. This claim seems to rest on either or both of the following assumptions. First, imparting of technical information relies less on verbal devices and makes use of non-verbal visual ones, and hence inadequacies of language do not matter as much as they would, say, for a course in political science or history. Second, whatever the linguistic inadequacies, they are of such a nature as not to hamper comprehension. None of these assumptions have been investigated in the Indian situation, but there have been investigations elsewhere, and we will refer to some of these. In the fifties, Noonan and Mackey (1953) reported that properly organized and implemented, a very small store of vocabulary can be effectively utilised for imparting instruction in science and mathematics. In general, educators consider the use of a second language as the medium of instruction as problematic in teaching and learning. Caroll (1961), Macnamara (1966), Ramos, Aguilar and Sibayan (1967), Cooper (1971), Collison (1974) and Goh (1973) indicate that using a second language as the medium of instruction is detrimental to students. On the other hand, admininstrators and politicians consider the use of a second language as the medium of instruction as beneficial, at least for a certain period. There are studies like those of Malherbe (1964) and Lambert and Tucker (1972), which report that learning other subjects through a second language might not be detrimental. Ho (1982), in a study exploring the relationship between achievement in physics and the medium of instruction, found that when students and teachers were sufficiently proficient in English, a second language for all, there was no significant difference in achievement when compared to a similar group receiving instruction through Chinese, their mother tongue. The crucial factor appears to be the level of proficiency in English. Beyond a particular level, the second language ceases to be problematic. But if students do not have a high level of proficiency, either in terms of accuracy or in terms of fluency (Brumfit 1984), then the use of a second language as the medium of instruction, will cause problems of comprehension and hamper the formation of scientific concepts. Since such concepts form the bases on which technical education is rooted, the latter is likely to be adversely effected if concepts are not understood and grasped.

At almost all levels of technical education (except in the Industrial Training Institute) English is the medium of instruction and lecturing is the usual mode. Some of the abilities needed to follow and make use of lectures are the following :

1. Guessing the meaning and use of unfamiliar lexical items through contextual clues.

2. Understanding the use of reference devices.
3. Understanding relations of various sections : focus and theme.
4. Recognising indicators in discourse for transition to another idea.
5. Recognising indicators in discourse for concluding an idea.
6. Understanding cohesion devices and hence the logical structure.
7. Distinguishing main ideas from supporting details.
8. Reducing the text through rejecting redundant use.

(Clarke and Leather 1980)

In India lectures in general reflect written discourse, which is "didactic" in nature, and which the students somehow need to be able to recognise and handle. The vocabulary is mostly technical, thus belonging to "non-spontaneous concepts" (Vygoatsky 1962). It is in this respect that the non-native student receiving technical instruction through English is at his greatest disadvantage. For assimilation, non-spontaneous concepts must assume a previous possession of spontaneous concepts (those derived through exposure to experience in non-formal everyday contexts of life) to provide an assimilatory framework. Indian learners, being non-native speakers of English, do not possess this framework in English. Hence, though the possession of specialised vocabulary is essential for the technical student in India, the means for absorbing these are not available. As a result, there is a great dependence on the verbal context, which leearners are unable to utilise because of their inadequate level of proficiency in the language. Hence ideational fluency and associated fluency of expression are greatly hindered.

As a rule it is assumed that learners comprehend concepts but cannot express them in English. It is suggested that lack of expression entails not expression alone, but comprehension of concepts as well. If this view is accurate, then it is clear that the role of language in technical education has been greatly underestimated and ignored.

Lecturing as a Tool for Instruction :

The purported aims of lectures are to provide information, promote thinking or teach/change attitudes. The objectives of technical education emphasize flexibility, initiative and thus indirectly, the processes of thinking. By stressing the life-long nature of technical education, these also recognise the ability for "learning to learn" as a desirable one. The focus on developing broad based abilities of judgement, decision making, problem solving and extrapolation render the older concept of transfer of knowledge inappropriate for achieving the goals of technical education. As lectures are notoriously ineffective tools either for promoting thinking or for changing attitudes (Bligh 1972), the use of lectures in English cannot be considered adequate for technical education. Further, lectures cannot help in developing the various skills of communication which are so essential for technical personnel.

Writing Needs for Technical Students :

Table 5.4 below shows the writing needs of technical students.

Table 5.4
Showing Technical Students' Writing Needs

Study Related Writing	Examination Related Writing	Writing Related Functions
Reports	Preparing Questions	Description
Laboratory Notes	Answering Questions	Estimate of materials
Taking Notes		Calculations for Problmes
		Design and Project Work
		Proposals
		Justifications
		Arguments

Within industry English is used mostly for written communication. This comprises letters, enquiries, notices, instructions, maintenance of records, reports, departmental notes, applications, estimates, drawings, operation schedules, complaints, securing orders, project proposals, works order, job cards, design and layout for products, purchase forms, purchase orders, shop indents, standard procedures, price negotiations, justification of order, memos and circulars and so on.

Spoken Communication : Spoken English is usually taken to mean conversation. However, spoken English which needs to be used in industry and for technical education, does not mean conversation in its ordinary sense. Within technical education understanding spoken English involves asking questions and responding to questions. In industry spoken English involves negotiations of various kinds, entailing persuading, suggesting, convincing, agreeing, disagreeing, handling complaints, complaining and the like. All these involve the use of English as a tool or as a means of doing something. Obviously, the need for the learner is to be aware of these various functions of language and perform these through English. In the present context of globalisation and market economy such functions assume a crucial role.

If English needs to be used in the ways indicated, can the traditional syllabuses in English provide these skills to the learners? Judging by the proficiency in English displayed by the average secondary student from regional medium schools, the answer appears to be negative. In that case such skills cannot be assumed to be part of the polytechnic student's repertoire, but need to be developed along with his technical knowledge. This calls for a language syllabus innovative both in content and methodology, so that necessary skills for written and spoken communication can be adequately developed. Setting out the details of such a syllabus is outside the scope of the present book (Datta 1986), but it must be remembered that language plays a significant role in technical education.

Notes :

1. The problem encompasses much more than the problem of lexis, technical and quasi technical.

2. Research reported by Ho (1982) and Hewson and Hewson (1983) for Chinese and African students respectively and Cantieni and Tremblay (1975) for the development of mathematical and language concepts.

3. *The Literature of the English Renaissance*, 1485-1600. Vol. II in a *History of English Literature* by Hardin Craig, London, Collier Macmillan Ltd, 1962 : 215.

4. This is exemplified in the efforts of the four TTTIs to produce text books for English as a subject for polytechnics.

5. If Helen Bernard (1961) is to be believed, these students are not

likely to have a word store of more than 1500 words in English.

6. The contrast is between traditional covering of knowledge and innovative, unusual techniques, between lectures and demonstrations, lectures and laboratory experimentation.

7. In practice subject teachers in polytechnics for example, appear to make a number of adjustments for facilitating student comprehension; e.g. use of the mother tongue when English fails, dictating of notes when students are unable to make sense of recommended textbooks.

6

The Present Socio-Economic Context of North-East India

In order to understand how technical education has worked in the North East and how it needs to be utilised for the material and economic development of the region, it is necessary to consider the present socio-economic context of the area. The present chapter is concerned with this task.

The North-East is an umbrella term used to denote the so-called "seven sisters" : the states of Arunachal Pradesh, Assam, Manipur, Meghalaya, Mizoram, Nagaland and Tripura, having collective borders with Bangladesh, Bhutan, Burma and Tibet/China. The seven states together account for 7.7 per cent of the geographical area of the country and 3.73 (1991) per cent of the population. The density of population varies from 286 persons per square km in Assam to 10 in Arunachal Pradesh, the overall density being 123, against the all India figure of 273. In overall terms then, the area is sparsely populated. The reason for this lies in topography and vegetation. Nearly seventy percent of the region is hilly and nearly 88 percent of the population live in the villages. In essence then, the area is predominantly rural, the mainstay being agriculture. About 209 tribes are indegenous to the region.

In other words, this is an area which is multilingual, multicultural, multiethnical and multireligious in nature. The living styles, incomes, food habits, cultivation practices, ways of worship, birth and death rituals, marriage customs, cultural mores, land ownership and the like, all display an immense variety, as do the topographical features of hills, valleys, rivers and forests. Further, the existing life styles and practices indicate the agrarian nature of the communities and the obvious absence of heavy industries. Establishing of heavy industries, as appears to be the aim of the existing science and technological policies, will tend to change the existing demographic, environmental and socilogical pattern, not to speak of work-habits, leading to drastic changes in the social set-up. Because of such potential changes, the subsequent economic and material growth is neither directly measureable, nor directly computable. In other words, it is not possible to predict with any certainty that the setting up of a particular industry will benefit the society in question in a particular manner. Hence the planning for growth and development by providing technical education is not a simple matter of direct calculation.

Available Natural Resources :

In such a context one of the more certain parameters for consideration is the availability of existing natural and human resources and the state of the use of the same. Another aspect is the possible or potential development of a particular resource.

In a country like India, human resource is the most basic one. In the North-East the changing demographic pattern has become a very sensitive issue. The growth of population, the shifting ratio between various groups and the changing balance of power have led to political and ethnic turbulances, influencing development and growth.

In the sections that follow, the existing socio-economic profile will be considered. Table 6.1 shows the districtwise divisions of the various states as on September 1991, and underscores the predominantly rural character of the region.

Table 6.1
Administrative Division of N E States

State	District (As on 01.01.92)	Panchayats (As on 01.09.91)	Blocks (As on 31.03.92)	Villages (1981 Census)	Towns (1991)
1	2	3	4	5	6
Arunachal Pradesh	11	860	54	3,257	10
Assam	23	2,162	206	21,995	93
Manipur	8	166	31	2,035	31
Meghalaya	5	-	30	4,902	12
Mizoram	3	622 *	20	721	22
Nagaland	7	980 *	28	1,112	9
Tripura	3	911	18	856	18
Total	60	5,701	387	34,878	195
All India	478	2,21,754	5,239	5,79,132	4,689

* Traditional Council of Village elders.

Sources : Census of India 1991 - Series -1/Ministry of Rural Development.

Source : Basic statistics of the North Eastern Region, 1995.

Table 6.2 shows the percentage of urban population in the region. Except for Manipur and Mizoram, this percentage in much below the all India figure.

Table 6.2
Distribution of Population by Area - 1991

State	Total	Rural	Urban	Percentage of Urban Population
1	2	3	4	5
Arunachal Pradesh	864,558	753,930	110,628	12.80
Assam	22,414,322	19,926,527	2,487,795	11.10
Manipur	1,837,149	1,331,504	505,645	27.52
Meghalaya	1,774,778	1,444,731	330,047	18.60
Mizoram	6,89,756	3,71,810	3,17,946	46.10
Nagaland	1,209,546	1,001,323	208,223	17.21
Tripura	2,757,205	2,335,484	421,721	15.30
Total	31,547,314	27,165,309	4,382,005	13.89
All India	846,302,688	628,691,676	217,611,012	26.13

Source : Census of India 1991, Series - 1 ; Paper - 2 of 1992.
From : Basic statistics of the North Eastern Region, 1995

Available Natural Resources and the Level of their Utilisation :

The North Eastern region is blessed by the bounty of mother nature. Water, forest, wood and agricultural produce and various minerals are found in plenty, although the distribution is uneven. The soil is in general fertile and the region receives abundant rainfall.

Forest :

The forest cover in the North Eastern region varies between 51% and 87% of the total land area in the various states, compared to the all India figure of 19.5%. The forests abound in both hard and soft wood trees. Nearly 25 percent of the forest has tropical vegetation. Bamboo and cane of different varieties grow abundantly. Thatch, grass and reed growing in abundance serve as housing materials. Different kinds of ferns, flowering plants, orchids, deciduous and evergreen forests grow in the region. However, the depletion of forest cover in recent years has been very rapid, mainly due to shifting cultivation. Other reasons like unplanned and over utilisation of natural forest resources aggravate the condition, reaching almost a point of no return.

Water :

The region receives very heavy rainfall and it rains almost all round the year. Rainfall ranges from 250 cm in the plains to 635 cm in the eastern hills between June and September. Mawsynram in Meghalaya is the wettest place on earth with an average annual rainfall of 11,900 mm.

There are numerous rivers, huge and small, in the region. Many carry only a trickle most of the time, but become swollen and flooded during in the rainy season. Most of the perennial rivers are subject to severe erosions. As a result, an enormous quantity of soil is washed away during the monsoon and is carried by the rivers, causing silting of river beds and raising them, flooding the adjoining crop land in the process.

Inspite of floods and easy access to ground water, there is an acute shortage of potable drinking water in the region. Supply of filtered water to towns and villages is an exception rather them the norm, highlighting a lack of proper infrastructure for purification and distribution.

Agriculture :

The main food crops and grains produced in the region include high yielding varieties of paddy and wheat, maize, pulses like gram and tur, oil seeds like ground nut, sesame, castorseed, rapeseed, mustard, linseed and sunflower, sugarcane, cotton and jute, potato, turmeric, ginger, soyabean, onion, chillies, tobacco, tapioca, sweet potato and areca nuts. Fruits like coconut, banana, pineapple, orange, lemon, lime, mango, guava, litchie, papaya, jackfruit, apple, peas, plum and peach are either cultivated in farms or grow indigenously. Among nuts, cashew nuts (Tripura) and walnuts (Arunachal Pradesh) are cultivated. Among vegetables, tomatoes, cabbages, cauliflower, squash, colcasia, brinjal, beans, potatoes and the like are grown. Tea is cultivated extensively. Rubber and coffee are also being grown now.

In measuring development in agriculture the use of fertilizers and the extent of irrigation are used as indices. Table 6.3 and 6.4 show such utilisation. Both fall much below the all India level and are indicators of the slower rate of development in the region.

Table 6.3
Shows Irrigated Area as Percentage of Sown Area for Foodgrains and for all Crops in 1990-91

000 Hectares

State	Sown area (foodgrains)	Irrigated area	%	Sown area (all crops)	Irrigated area	%
Arunachal Pradesh	189	32	16.92	247	32	12.96
Assam	2727	538	19.73	3797	572	15.06
Manipur	162	75	46.30	180	75	41.67
Meghalaya	135	47	34.81	243	47	19.34
Mizoram	58	8	13.79	74	8	10.81
Nagaland	181	59	32.60	210	60	28.57
Tripura	291	34	11.68	445	41	9.21
All India			34.56			33.31

Source : Basic Statistics of North Eastern Region 1995.

Further, canal systems for irrigation are very few in number. Most prevalent is the system of minor irrigation.

Table 6.4
Details of Inland Water Resources

	Length in Kms		Lakhs Hectares	
States	Rivers and Canals	Reservoirs	Tanks and Ponds	Beels, Lakes and Derelict Water
Arunachal Pradesh	2000		0.01	0.03
Assam	4820	0.55	0.20	1.10
Manipur	3360	Neg	0.03	0.29
Meghalaya	1000	0.01	0.02	Neg
Mizoram	1748	-	0.02	-
Nagaland	1600	0.27	0.50	Neg
Tripura	1200	0.06	0.07	0.06
All India	1,64,121	19.73	22.12	12.96

Neg - negligible

Source : Basic Statisticss of North Eastern Region 1995.

Table 6.5 Indicates the use of various kinds of fertilizers in the region.

Table 6.5
Showing Total Consumption of Nitrogen, Phosphate and Potash for 1993-94

000 Tonnes

State	Nitrogen (N)	Phosphate (P_2O_5)	Potash (K_2O)
Arunachal Pradesh	0.28	0.21	0.08
Assam	20.44	4.78	4.29
Manipur	8.35	1.08	0.18
Meghalaya	1.88	0.94	0.54
Mizoram	0.42	0.55	0.18
Nagaland	0.49	0.46	0.14
Tripura	4.56	2.90	2.50
All India	8986.11	2.883.99	962.55

Source : Planning Commission

Table 6.6 shows the consumption of plant nutrients per unit of grass cropped area for the year 1992-93.

Table 6.6

(Kg/Hect)

State	N	P_2O_5	K_2O	Total
Arunachal Pradesh	1.2	0.6	0.2	2.0
Assam	4.2	1.3	1.4	6.9
Manipur	36.3	10.3	3.2	49.8
Meghalaya	6.5	5.1	0.8	12.4
Mizoram	5.6	7.5	3.3	16.4
Nagaland	1.4	1.9	3.0	3.7
Tripura	12.2	6.0	3.0	21.3
All India	46.5	15.7	4.9	67.1

Source : Basic Statistics of NER 1995.

In order to help agriculturalists in the utilisation of fertilizers, soil testing laboratories have been set up and Mobile Soil Testing Vans are used. Table 6.7 provide a picture of the utilisation of such facilities.

Table 6.7
State-wise number of Soil Testing Laboratories Analysing Capacity and Capacity Utilisation as on 31.3.90

State	No. of Soil testing labs	Annual analysing capacity (1000 nos)	Capacity Utilisation (per cent) 1986-87	No. of districts not yet having soil testing labs
Arunachal Pradesh	1	5	52	9
Assam	13(8)	84	60	4
Manipur	1(-)	15	38	5
Meghalaya	1(1)	8	83	2
Mizoram	1(1)	5	72	2
Nagaland	1(1)	10	NA	6
Tripura	2(1)	10	95	2
All India	462(89)	6625	84	112

Figures in brackets indicate the number of mobile vans
Source : Basic Statistics of NER 1995.

Livestock and Poultry :

Tables 6.8 and 6.9 show the production of milk, eggs, fish and livestock.

Table 6.8

State	Milk (000 Tonnes) 1990-91	Egg (Lakh number) 1990-91	Fish (000 tonnes) 1990-91
Arunachal Pradesh	41	310	1.25
Assam	653	5,000	76.00
Manipur	82	920	8.50
Meghalaya	48	660	1.52
Mizoram	8	20	2.95
Nagaland	43	400	0.83
Tripura	29	340	21.20

Source : Basic Statistics of NER 1995.

An idea of the livestock and poultary resources can be had from Table 6.9

Table 6.9
(Livestock census 1987)

(In thousands)

State	Cattle	Buffa-loes	Sheep	Goats	Horses and Ponies	Pigs	Yaks	Total Poultry
Arunachal Pradesh	311	12	28	108	5	243	8	1121
Assam	7278	623	67	2134	14	642	-	11451
Manipur	770	141	16	44	1	383	-	3018
Meghalaya	587	28	15	194	5	280	-	1590
Mizoram	50	5	1	20	2	82	-	838
Nagaland	203	15	1	72	-	314	-	1124
Tripura	828	16	3	441	1	89	-	1865
All India	198567	76769	44837	99405	782	10760	36	258335

Source : Basic Statistics of NER 1995.

In general the milk yield is low. Hence hybridization is made mainly through artificial insemination. For this purpose intensive Cattle development Project, goat, pig and sheep farms have been set up in various states. Veterinary hospitals, dispensaries and polyclinics have also been set up. The setting up of dairies have helped in the production, collection and distribution of milk and paneer.

Electricity :

Though the North Eastern region has an immerse potential for producing electricity specially from hydel sources, factors like the absence of infrastructure, lack of communication and difficult topograpy have hindered adequate generation, utilisation and distribution of such power. Table 6.10 shows the installed and effective capacity of power as on 31-3-94.

Table 6.10
Installed and Effective Capacity of Power as on 31-3-94.

(In MW)

State	Hydel	Thermal and GT	Diesel	Total	Effective Capacity
Arunachal Pradesh	22.95	-	14.65	37.58	36.41
Assam	2.00	534.50	20.69	557.19	532.40
Manipur	2.80	-	9.27	12.07	10.21
Meghalaya	186.71	5.00	2.05	193.76	187.66
Mizoram	3.38	-	19.07	22.45	19.88
Nagaland	2.50	-	3.62	6.12	5.36
Tripura	16.00	32.50	6.14	54.64	54.64
Central Sector	255.00	-	-	255.00	255.00
Total for NE Region	491.34	572.00	75.47	1138.81	1101.56

Source : Basic statistics of NER 1995.

The per capita consumption of electricity in the region, as shown in table 6.11, is far below the all India level of consumption indicating the absence of heavy industries, and non use of consumer goods. It perhaps shows the persistence of the traditional life style where utmost use is made of daylight for one's activities.

Table 6.11
Percentage consumption of Electricity

(KWLH)

State	1988-89	1989-90	1992-93
Arunachal Pradesh	55	58	128.3
Assam	63	78	91.0
Manipur	57	80	140.4
Meghalaya	98	108	159.4
Mizoram	49	57	126.1
Nagaland	67	70	100.0
Tripura	41	51	83.9
All India	216	236	330.6

From : Basic statistics of NER 1995.

Housing :

Housing in the region is classified into Pucca, semi-pucca and kutcha (serviceable and unserviceable). Table 6.12 shows the distribution as in 1981.

Table 6.12
Percentage Distribution of Residential Houses by Type of Structure : 1981

State		Pucca	Semi Pucca	Serviceable Kutcha	Unserviceable Kutcha
Arunachal Pradesh	R	7.3	21.0	0.5	71.2
	U	47.8	17.3	1.3	33.6
Assam	R	-	-	-	-
	U	-	-	-	-
Manipur	R	1.7	23.4	16.0	58.9
	U	11.8	37.6	13.0	37.6
Meghalaya	R	10.5	25.4	3.2	60.9
	U	26.7	52.3	1.4	19.6
Mizoram	R	5.0	18.6	0.3	76.1
	U	49.0	27.2	0.1	23.7
Nagaland	R	5.9	23.7	1.0	69.4
	U	57.2	19.3	0.7	22.8
Tripura	R	40.6	43.7	12.2	4.1
	U	21.0	9.3	8.5	45.3
All India	R	22.4	42.2	22.6	12.8
	U	64.7	24.3	6.6	4.4

Source : National Building Organization
R = Rural U = Urban - = Not available

The predominance of unserviceable kutcha houses, specially in the rural areas indicate the economic condition of the population. In addition, there is an acute shortage of housing as shown in table 6.13.

Table 6.13
Statewise Estimate of Housing shortage : 1990

(Thousand)

State	Rural	Urban	Total
Arunachal Pradesh	59	-	59
Assam	3,665	312	3,977
Manipur	-	35	35
Meghalaya	216	-	216
Nagaland	120	-	120
Tripura	156	59	3,025*

From : Basic Statistics of NER 1995 (*This does not add up)

Compaנd to the rest of India, the shortage is negligible. However, the quality of houses and the facilities available leave a lot to be desired.

Health and Medical Care :

The state of health care in the region can be inferred from the per capita expenditure, the doctor population ratio, and the number of hospital beds available. Tables 6.14 and 6.15 show the ratio and the beds available, respectively.

Table 6.14
Statewise Number of Doctors and Doctor - Population Ratio, 1991

State	Doctors engaged under govt. agency	Population served per doctor	Period to which data relates
Arunachal Pradesh	233	1 : 3536	31.12.90
Assam	2.660	1 : 8750	31.12.91
Manipur	684	1 : 2675	31.12.91
Meghalaya	322	1 : 5357	31.12.90
Mizoram	146	1 : 5000	31.12.91
Nagaland	202	1 : 5401	31.12.89
Tripura	673	1 : 3822	31.12.90
All India	39.466		

From : Basic statistics of NER 1995.

Table 6.15

Number of Hospitals and Beds (as on 1 January 1992)

State	Rural		Urban		Total	
	Hospital	Beds	Hospital	Beds	Hospital	Beds
Arunachal Pradesh (1.1.91)	12	506	6	585	18	1,091
Assam (1.1.91)	151	3,949	117	8,712	268	12,661
Manipur (1.1.91)	21	765	4	695	25	1460
Meghalaya	0	0	8	1635	8	1635
Mizoram	4	136	10	992	14	1128
Nagaland (1.1.91)	21	321	10	793	31	1114
Tripura	10	275	13	1256	23	1531
All India	3,568	126,474	7,606	515,729	11,174	642,103

From : Basic statistics of NER 1995

Though 88 percent of the population live in villages, hospital bed facilities are greater in number in the urban area. This means that often critically sick people have to travel long distances over difficult terrain before getting medical facilities. The aim of bringing doctors and even basic health care within easy reach of people has not been fulfilled. This is another index of the phase/stage of development the area is in. Further the minimum number of population served by one doctor is 2675 while the highest in 8750.

Table 6.16 shows the per capita expenditure on health.

Table 6.16

Total and Per Capita State Government Expenditure on Health (1989-90)

State	Total Expenditure (Rs. in Crores)	Per capita Expenditures
Arunachal Pradesh	26	327
Assam	172	70
Manipur	37	219
Meghalaya	47	277
Mizoram	30	434
Nagaland	63	574
Tripura	40	161

Source : Basic statistics of NER 1995

Other Sources of Power :

Renewable energy technologies installations are found in all the states. These include various types of biogas plants, biomass gasifiers, improved chulas, solar photovoltaics for street lighting, solar pumps, community lighting systems, domestic lighting and TV system and power plants and urjasram water heating systems. These are ecofriendly, maintenance free and runs on available resources, but are expensive to instal.

Transport and Communication :

During earlier times, rivers provided the cheapest and convenient means of transport for man and goods. In the nineteenth century, rail tracks were laid in Assam. The first of these was laid in 1885 between Dibrugarh and Saikhowa Ghat and then from Makum to Ledo. The railway was connected to the riverport of Dibrugarh from where tea, coal, petroleum, timber and other products were carried by steamer to Calcutta. The longer Assam Bengal Railway was constructed in 1905, linking Tinsukia to the seaport of Chittagong (now in Bangladesh), via Lumding. Later it was linked to Calcutta via Guwahati. After independence a link railway line was constructed through the Siliguri corridor bypassing East Pakistan. The building of the Farakka Barrage over the Ganges, of a road-cum-railway bridge over Brahmaputra at Pandu and the conversion of meter gauge lines to broad gauge have eased rail communication with the rest of India.

However, as Table 6.17 will show, the rail tracks are unevenly distributed among the states.

Table 6.17
Railway Network in NER (as on 1992-93)

(In Km)

State	Broad Gauge (BG)	Meter Gauge(MG)	Narrow Gauge(NG)	Total Gauge
Arunachal Pradesh	-	1	-	1
Assam	266.41	2200.49	-	2466.83
Manipur	-	1	-	1
Meghalaya	-	-	-	-
Mizoram	-	2	-	2
Nagaland	-	9	-	9
Tripura	-	45	-	45
Total	266.41	2258.41	-	2524.83
All India	36504	21997	3985	62486

From : Basic Statistics of NER 1995

Roads form the main link within the North Eastern Region. Table 6.18 shows the existing road length.

Table 6.18
Road Length (as on 31.3.92)

(In Km)

State	Total Length	Sur-faced	Unsur-faced	Road per 100 sq.km.	Road per 000 popula-tion	% of surfa-ced road to total road length
Arunachal Pradesh	7520	2496	5024	8.9	8.77	33.19
Assam	68913	10841	58072	87.8	3.69	15.73
Manipur	6765	2741	4024	30.3	3.70	40.52
Meghalaya	7832	2931	4901	34.9	4.45	37.43
Mizoram	3705	1265	2440	17.6	5.37	34.19
Nagaland	8805	6842	1963	53.1	7.21	77.70
Tripura	13005	4448	8560	124.1	4.74	34.9
Total	116551	31567	84984	45.69	3.73	27.08
All India	2065209	1043365	1021844	62.8	2.44	50.52

From : Basic Statistics of NER 1995.

As can be seen at a glance, the road network is not adequate in many states. Moreover a large number of roads is unsurfaced, indicating that travelling by road is not easy.

A number of roads have the status of National Highways, and often are the only links for the landlocked states. These life lines are often subjected to insurgency related disturbances, bundhs and road blocks of one kind or another, and during the monsoon, frequent land slides. As a result, movement of traffic is often uncertain and gets suspended. Such breaks in the continuous flow of man and materials is quite common and indicate that the stage of communication is not sophisticated enough to function smoothly and without drawing attention to itself. Instead of being a means or a tool for development, it becomes a constraint.

Postal Services and Telecommunications :

These form a vital section of an overall communication system.

Inspite of air, rail and road links, postal services in the region are notoriously slow. Even speed posts lose their speed over the hilly terrain. Table 6.19 shows the number of post offices, population per post office and the area served by a post office. As is evident, the facilities are spread rather thin. Further, the functioning is rather tardy.

Table 6.19
Post Offices in NE Region (as on 1992-93)

State	Post Office (Number)			Population per post office	Area served by a post office (sq km)
	Total	Rural	Urban		
Arunachal Pradesh	269	256	13	2976	311.15
Assam	3780	3480	300	6772	22.31
Manipur	660	625	35	2727	33.33
Meghalaya	470	439	31	3836	44.65
Mizoram	362	323	39	1934	58.00
Nagaland	294	275	19	4082	56.11
Tripura	689	640	49	3774	15.08
All India	152037	135754	16283	5607	21.60

From : Basic Statistics of NER 1995

In general, the number of telephones in the area is on the rise. But there are many parts, specially rural, where a telephone is not easily within reach. Telegraph offices are also few in number, since not all post offices have this facility. E-mail, fax facilities and Telex services are in general not easily accessible to the common man. If easy communication is the basis of growth and development, then it can be said that this foundation is not available in the region.

Literacy and Education :

The total literacy rate in the North East is higher than the all India rate of 36.23%. However, except in Nagaland and Mizoram, the rate is less than 50%. The female literacy rate is also not very high. Table 6.20 below shows this.

Table 6.20
Percentage of Literacy to Total Population

State	Total (T) Rural (R) Urban (U)	Persons	Males	Females
1	2	3	4	5
Arunachal Pradesh	T	32.87	42.26	23.03
	R	29.41	37.95	19.68
	U	57.73	64.16	49.20
Assam	T	43.20	50.62	35.18
	R	39.96	47.53	31.88
	U	69.19	74.17	63.26
Manipur	T	49.00	58.24	39.40
	R	44.76	53.73	38.67
	U	60.11	70.10	40.81
Meghalaya	T	39.15	41.72	36.45
	R	32.60	34.95	30.14
	U	67.68	70.34	64.74
Mizoram	T	67.36	70.36	64.11
	R	58.39	62.40	54.01
	U	77.81	79.82	75.76
Nagaland	T	51.09	56.04	45.52
	R	47.60	52.82	41.87
	U	67.82	70.49	64.42
Tripura	T	49.86	58.23	41.01
	R	45.83	54.93	35.83
	U	72.24	76.67	67.61
All India	T	36.23	46.89	24.82
	R	29.65	40.79	17.96
	U	57.40	65.83	47.82

Source : Provisional Population Totals, Paper-I of 1991 Supplement, Arunachal Pradesh.

From : Basic Statistics of NER 1995, p. 136.

Table 6.21 shows the budgeted expenditure on education.

Table 6.21
Budgeted Expenditure on Education

State	Per Capita Budgeted Expenditure (Rs) 1991-92	Percentage of Budgeted Expenditure on Education to Total Budget 1991-92
Arunachal Pradesh	512.50	14.63
Assam	217.41	24.33
Manipur	433.93	26.49
Meghalaya	436.81	20.36
Mizoram	670.75	15.43
Nagaland	605.55	16.25
Tripura	453.83	22.13
All India	243.92	13.33

From : Basic Statistics of NER 1995.

The per capita expenditure and percentage of the state budget on education is much higher than the all India figure. However, there is a general feeling that barring some pockets, the quality of education is not very high. Even at the school level a large number of students go out of the region for their studies. This indicates the general lack of trust on the credibility of education.

Table 6.22 shows the number of educational institutions in the North Eastern region.

Table 6.22
Number of Educational Institutions (As on September 1992)

(Numbers)

Institution	Arunachal Pradesh	Assam	Manipur	Meghalaya	Mizoram	Nagaland	Tripura
1	2	3	4	5	6	7	8
University	1	3	1	1	*	8	1
Board of Secondary Education	-	2	1	1	1	1	1
Art/Science and Commerce Colleges	4	217@	31	23	12@	16	14
Engineering Colleges	-	3	-	-	-	-	1
Medical Colleges	-	3@	1+	-	-	-	-
Agriculture Colleges	-	2	1	-	-	1	-
Veterinary Colleges	-	1	-	-	-	-	-
Teacher Training Colleges	-	9@	3+	1	1@	1	1
Junior Colleges (+2 stage)	-	16@	10+	-	3	5	-
Higher Secondary Schools (10+2 pattern)	55	367@	33	2	-	-	148
High School	84	3,084@	453	314	273	189	331
Middle Schools	274	5,703	681	705	553	357	432
Primary School	1,171	28,876@	3,180	4,170	1,066	1,305	2,065
Pre-primary Schools	249	482@	1	1,165	-	-	2,513
Teachers Training Schools	-	33	2	10	2	4	2
Polytechnics	2	8@	1+	19	3	1	3 4
Technical and Industrial School	2	27@	19	3	1	3	4

Source :- Selected Educational Statistics, 1992-93, Ministry of Human Resource Development, Govt. of India, New Delhi.

* : Campus of NEHU at nagaland and Mizoram.

@ Relates to 1991-92.

Banking :

Table 6.23 shows the areawise branches of banks and the average population served by each bank.

Table 6.23
Areawise Bank Branches (as on 30.9.94)

State	R (Rural)	SU (Semi Urban)	U (Urban)	T (Total)	Average population per Bank
Arunachal Pradesh	75	-	22	97	8,916
Assam	879	261	153	1293	17,335
Manipur	58	9	18	85	21,612
Meghalaya	140	29	42	211	8,412
Mizoram	73	5	11	89	7,753
Nagaland	51	45	-	96	12,599
Tripura	132	20	29	181	15,232

From : Basic Statistics of NER, 1995.

This is an indication of the inadequate number of banks in the area. Banks are neither easily accessible nor are many facilities available. The record of loan recovery is dismal, banks often having to write off loans given for setting up of units for self employment. Such unrealised loans are indicative of the lack of entrepreneurship in the region.

Table 6.24 below provides a picture of the composite index of backwardness on all India basis.

Table 6.24
Composite Index of Backwardness

State	SC/ST Population 1981	Relative Shares	Agricultural labours in 1981	Relative Shares	Weighted (combined relative shares
Arunachal Pradesh	444086	0.2779	7796	0.0139	0.1459
Assam	3430150	2.1463	552048	0.9849	1.5656
Manipur	405730	0.2539	28613	0.0510	0.1525
Meghalaya	1081837	0.6769	57899	0.103	0.3901
Mizoram	462042	0.2891	5118	0.0091	0.1491
Nagaland	650885	0.4073	2979	0.0053	0.2063
Tripura	844304	0.5596	146089	0.2606	0.4101
All India	159813411		56051743		

From : Basic Statistics of NER, 1995.

Economic Census :

Table 6.25 is concerned with the number of persons usually working in the various enterprises in the organised sector.

Table 6.25
Establishment and Employment in the Organised Sector in NE Region (as on 1.1.88)

State	Establishment (Nos)			Employment (Thousands)		
	Public Sector	Private Sector	Total	Public Sector	Private Sector	Total
Assam	4,606	1,654	6,260	453.0	492.2	945.2
Manipur	502	20	522	48.3	0.4	48.7
Meghalaya	613	136	749	56.3	4.6	60.8
Mizoram	437	16	453	27.1	1.2	28.3
Nagaland	587	111	698	66.0	1.6	67.7
Tripura	177	242	419	86.7	9.0	89.7

From : Basic Statistics of NER 1995.

In the next Table, that is Table 6.26, the number of total enterprises and number of persons usually working by sex, is shown.

Table 6.26
Number of Total Enterprises and Number of Persons usually working by Sex

State	Enterprise			Persons usually working		
	Total*	Agril	Non Agril	Total	Male	Female
Arunachal Pradesh	21,461	1,429	20,032	95,576	83,411	12,165
Assam	4,80,622	23,794	4,56,828	13,25,547	11,66,012	1,59,435
Manipur	60,399	5,019	55,380	1,55,135	1,00,996	54,139
Meghalaya	49,973	2,827	47,146	1,66,007	1,25,210	40,797
Mizoram	23,246	1,264	21,982	87,792	60,021	27,771
Nagaland	23,310	1,851	21,459	93,771	75,697	18,074
Tripura	83,758	3,473	80,283	2,14,315	1,84,773	29,546

*Excludes Crop Production and Plantation
From : Basic Statistics of NER, 1995.

Of these enterprises, some operate without premises and some without power, showing the lack of proper infrastructural facilities. Table 6.27 indicates these features. Of these, the majority is in rural areas.

Table 6.27
Number of Total Enterprises with Selected Principal Characteristics

State	Number of Enterprises*			
	Without Premises	Perennial	Without Power	Owned by Private
Arunachal Pradesh	2,124	20,123	15,705	15,114
Assam	64,143	4,54,763	3,95,474	3,65,357
Manipur	12,839	55,380	51,611	56,086
Meghalaya	8,701	48,165	40,319	42,132
Mizoram	4,234	21,802	19,356	16,523
Nagaland	1,884	21,290	16,934	17,557
Tripura	17,209	81,037	68,606	71,717

* Excludes Crop production and plantation
From : Basic Statistics of NER, 1995

Utilisation of Resources (Industries) :

The various industries of the region can be categorised in various ways. One possibility is to distinguish them by size. Table 6.28 and 6.29 indicate the large and medium scale and small scale industries in the region respectively.

Table 6.28
Large and Medium Scale Industries in North Eastern Region (As on 31 March, 1994)

State	No. of Units	Percentage
1	2	3
Arunachal Pradesh	17	5.8
Assam	118	74.8
Manipur	6	3.9
Meghalaya	7	4.5
Mizoram	1	0.0
Nagaland	16	10.4
Tripura	1	0.6
Total	166	100.0

Source : NISIET; Guwahati.
From : Basic Statistics of NER 1995

Table 6.29
Trend of Development of SSI in different States of N.E. Region (1971-1988)

State	1971	1981	1985	1986	1987	1988*
1	2	3	4	5	6	7
Arunachal Pradesh		189	262	213	278	374
		(1.9)	(1.9)	(1.3)	(1.8)	(1.8)
Assam	809	4,153	6,543	7,362	8,727	10,210
	(81.6)	(42.3)	(47.4)	(44.8)	(44.1)	(50.1)
Manipur	8	3,422	3,157	4,220	4,830	2,892
	(0.8)	(34.8)	(12.9)	(25.7)	(24.4)	(14.2)
Meghalaya	-	233	571	643	762	1,000
	-	(2.4)	(4.1)	(3.9)	(3.9)	(4.9)
Mizoram	-	298	826	1,191	1,566	1,866E
	-	(3.0)	(6.0)	(7.9)	(9.2)	(9.2)
Nagaland	-	345	395	431	471	509
	-	(3.5)	(2.9)	(2.6)	(2.4)	(2.5)
Tripura	174	1,183	2,062	2,392	3,136	3,523
	(17.6)	(12.0)	(14.9)	(14.5)	(15.9)	(17.3)
N.E. Region	991	9,823	13,816	16,452	19,770	20,377
	(100)	(100)	(100)	(100)	(100)	(100)
All India	2,39,128	5,23,180	8,54,843	9,50,334	10,48,253	11,58,765

Note : Figures in brackets indicate percentage, *=Provisional, E=Estimated
Source : NISIET; Guwahati
From : Basic Statistics of NER, 1995.

Another possibility is to classify industries by the raw materials these use. Such a classification would include :

A. Mineral - Based Industries like
   i) Coal
   ii) Petroleum
   iii) Natural Gas
   iv) Petrochemicals
   v) Fertilizers
   vi) Cement

B. Forest - Based Industries like
   i) Plywood
   ii) Paper
   iii) Matches

C. Crop - Based Industries like
   i) Tea
   ii) Coffee
   iii) Rubber
   iv) Sugar
   v) Tobacco

D. Fibre - Based Industries like
   i) Jute
   ii) Cotton
   iii) Coir
   iv) Sisal
   v) Silk and Spun silk

E. Oil - Based Industries like
   i) Mustard
   ii) Sesame
   iii) Linseed
   iv) Rape seed
   v) Groundnut
   vi) Soyabean.

In addition, cottage industry exists in the form of weaving and handicraft, bamboo and cane products, bell-metal, jewellery, pottery, food processing, bakery and the like.

Since Tea and Petroleum products are two most important industries in the region, more information regarding these are provided in the following tables.

Table 6.30
Tea

State	Number of Tea Estates 1991*	Area under Tea (Hectares) 1991*	Production of Tea (Thousand Kg.) 1993*
Arunachal Pradesh	9	560	50
Assam	848	236,811	402,947
Manipur	2	170	25
Nagaland	1	52	-
Tripura	58	6,000	5,607
All India	13,873	425,026	758,063

* Provisional

From : Basic Statistics of NER 1995.

Table 6.31
Production of Crude Oil and Natural Gas

State	Crude Oil (000 Tones) 1993-94	Natural Gas (Million Cubic Metres) 1993-94
Arunachal Pradesh	49	
Assam/Nagaland	5,090	2,025

From : Basic Statistics of NER 1995.

Table 6.32 shows the mineral production of the region.

Table 6.32

(Value : Rupees in thousand)

State	Minerals	1992-93 QTY (000 tonnes)	1992-93 Value
Arunachal Pradesh	Petroleum (crude)	59	1,58,208
	Limestone	1	41
Assam	Coal	1,101	6,66,495
	Natural Gas(utilised)	1,311	14,42,100
	Petroleum(crude)	4,986	1,31,93,237
	Limestone	188	15,883
Manipur	Chromite	158	95

Meghalaya	Sillimanite	620	2,740
	Limestone	164	10,450
Tripura	Natural Gas (utilised)	115	1,26,500

Natural gas in million cubic metre.
From : Basic Statistics of NER 1995.

The weaving of cloth is another important industry in the North Eastern region. Table 6.33 shows the powerloom in the area.

Table 6.33

State	Power Looms				Spinning Spindles		
	Autho-rised	In-stalled	Active	Idle	Mills	Autho-rised	In-stalled
Arunachal Pradesh	-	-	-	-	-	-	-
Assam	1,576	620	150	470	5	1,19,852	83,626
Manipur	32	3	1	2	1	25,488	16,416
Meghalaya	-	-	-	-	-	-	-
Mizoram	-	-	-	-	-	-	-
Nagaland	6	3	1	2	-	-	-
Tripura	24	3	1	2	-	-	-

From : Basic Statistics of NER 1995.

Table 6.34 provides a picture of the existence of handlooms in the region.

Table 6.34
Handloom in NER - 1988

(Hundred)

State	Total Looms	Commercial		Non-Commercial	
		Active	Idle	Active	Idle
Arunachal Pradesh	1,005	2	3	600	400
Assam	7,000	288	265	3,933	2,514
Manipur	3,000	855	45	1,260	840
Meghalaya	56	36	19	253	253
Mizoram	65	42	18	840	560
Nagaland	1,500	55	45	840	560
Tripura	1,100	65	35	800	200

From : Basic Statistics of NER 1995.

Table 6.35 shows the sericulture activities in the region for the year 1991-92.

Table 6.35
Sericulture in the North Eastern States

State	(Hect Area under Mulberry cultiva-tion	Produc-tion of Mulberry Cocoons Lakh Kgs	Produc-tion of Oak Tasar Reeling Lakh Nos	Produc-tion of Eri Cut Cocoons Lakh Kgs	(Hect) Produc-tion of Muga Reeling Lakh Nos
Arunachal Pradesh	50.00	0.156	1.57	0.118	2.94
Assam	1763.92	1.97	NA	4.995	3995.40
Manipur	15.750	3.52	20.97	3.79	NA
Meghalaya	1171.58	0.109	0.094	0.70	45.97
Mizoram	390	0.0014	2.13	0.014	0.068
Nagaland	140	0.14	9.25	0.45	2.15
Tripura	1325	0.451		NA	NA

From : Basic Statistics of NER 1995.

The overall health of the industrial scene can be judged by the number of sick and closed units. Table 6.36 is an attempt to do so for the North Eastern region.

Table 6.36
State wise Working/Closed Units in the NER

State	Working Units	Closed Units	Total	% of Closed Units
Arunachal Pradesh	326	36	362	9.94
Assam	4,430	1,732	6,162	28.11
Manipur	2,078	169	2,247	7.52
Meghalaya	587	136	723	18.81
Mizoram	917	306	1,223	25.02
Nagaland	183	83	266	31.20
Tripura	809	603	1,412	42.70
N.E. Region	9,330	3,065	12,396	24.72
All India	5,82,368	3,01,390	8,83,758	34.10

From : Basic Statistics of NER 1995.

Tourism in the region has an immense potential as it is rich in natural beauty and exotic flora and fauna. However, due to difficulties in communication, long duration of the rainy season, lack of amenities and other reasons, this industry has not been able to achieve its full potential. Further, the existence of the Innerline Permit system in some parts of the region is a deterrant to both foreign and domestic travellers. Table 6.37 provides a glimpse of the tourist flow to the region during 1988-89.

Table 6.37
Tourist flow in NER : 1988-89

State	Number		
	Domestic	Foreign	Total
Arunachal Pradesh			
Assam	3,01,275	1000	3,02,278
Manipur	77,549	109	77,658
Meghalaya	1,55,474	328	1,55,802
Mizoram	16,465	17	16,502
Nagaland	40,800	52	40,857
Tripura	NA	NA	NA

From : Basic Statistics of NER 1995.

In order to round off the economic picture, the per capita income at constant as well as current prices will be presented in Table 6.38 and 6.39 respectively. In real terms the change is not significant, an indication of the tardy development of the region. Further, the per capita income of the individual states and of the whole North-Eastern region is below the all India figure, indicating the overall level of development.

Table 6.38

Per Capita Netstate Domestic Product at Constant (1980-81) Prices

(Rupees)

State	1980-81	1981-82	1982-83	1983-84	1984-85	1985-86	1986-87	1987-88	1988-89	1989-90	1990-91	1991-92 (P)	1992-93 (Q)
1	2	3	4	5	6	7	8	9	10	11	12	13	14
Arunachal Pradesh	1561	1747	1744	1804	1908	2074	2133	2182	2360	2441	2452	2493	-
Assam	1200	1307	1367	1375	1457	1483	1474	1521	1516	1772	1805	1887	1945
Manipur	1429	1472	1457	1547	1571	1623	1618	1675	1723	1761	1850	2002	-
Meghalaya	1361	1379	1361	1354	1385	1412	1397	1485	1471	1610	1764	1906	1995
Nagaland	1448	1578	1720	1695	1681	1654	1768	1907	1975	1980	1894	1888	-
Tripura	1323	1311	1439	1354	1349	1335	1351	1480	1565	1628	1664	-	-
All India	1625	1692	1699	1804	1827	1857	1893	1929	2099	2201	2258	2225	2267

P : Provisional : Q : Quick Estimates

Source :- Central Statistical Organisation.

Table 6.39
Per Capita Netstate Domestic Product at Current Prices

(Rupees)

State	1980-81	1981-82	1982-83	1983-84	1984-85	1985-86	1986-87	1987-88	1988-89	1989-90	1990-91	1991-92 (P)	1992-93 (Q)
1	2	3	4	5	6	7	8	9	10	11	12	13	14
Arunachal Pradesh	1561	2011	2240	2455	2793	3274	3575	3680	4212	4467	5046	5551	-
Assam	1200	1474	1641	1777	2182	2313	2420	2589	2772	3589	4014	4594	5056
Manipur	1429	1682	1745	2020	2270	2362	2636	3040	3568	3674	3893	4180	-
Meghalaya	1361	1516	1626	1831	2047	2250	2479	2955	3118	3863	4530	5231	5769
Mizoram	1289	1383	1471	1724	2139	2658	3165	4077	4026	4135	-	-	-
Nagaland	1448	1704	1966	2203	2453	2591	2781	3385	3706	4333	5006	5863	-
Tripura	1323	1524	1638	1632	1942	2074	2123	2371	2991	3170	3430	-	-
All India	1625	1861	2013	2317	2523	2749	2986	3319	3898	4424	5054	5716	6380

P : Provisional : Q : Quick Estimates
Source :- Central Statistical Organisation.

A significant input to the economy of the region is central assistance, mainly in terms of plan outlay. Table 6.40 shows the extent of this assistance.

Table 6.40
Plan Outlay in N.E. Region
(Rs. in Crores)

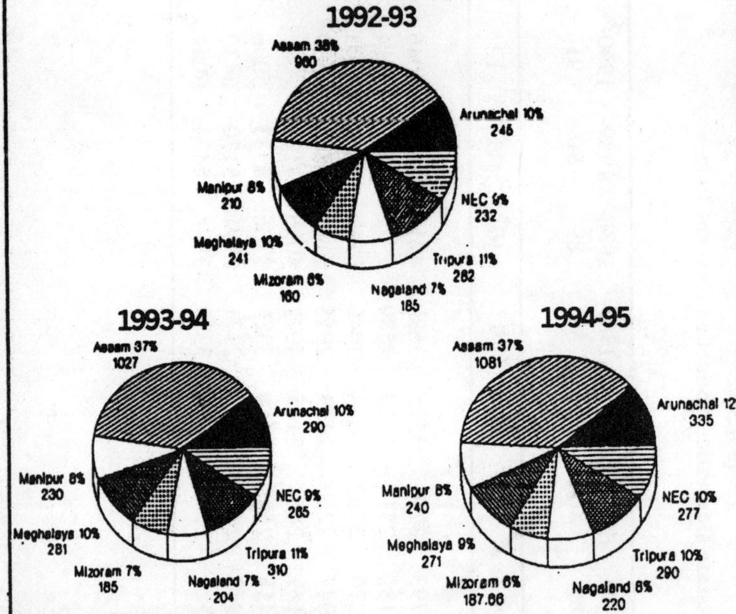

Source : Planning Commission

Table 6.41 on the next page shows the increase in the plan outlay for the succeeding Five year plans.

Table 6.42 provides a detailed break up of the Plan outlay for the year 1993-94.

These tables show very clearly that indigenous generation of revenue is not very significant in this region and this underscores the need for development in the region.

In this chapter an overall picture of the existing resources and their utilisation has been attempted, drawing attention to the gaps and lacuna that need to be rectified. In the next chapter possible suggestions for the same will be provided.

Table 6.41
Plan Outlay & Expenditure in NE Region

(Rs. in crores)

State	First Plan (1951-56)	Second Plan (1956-61)	Third Plan (1961-66)	Three Annual Plan (1966-69)	Fourth Plan (1969-74)	Fifth Plan (1974-79)	Annual Plan (1979-80)	Sixth Plan (1980-85)	Seventh Plan (1985-	Annual Plan 1990-91	1991-92	Eight Plan Total	(1992-93	(1993-94)	(1994-95)
1	2	3	4	5	6	7	8	9	10	11	12	13	14	15	16
Arunachal	4.21	9.51	7.15	8.57	17.99	63.30	23.41	212.00	400.00	183.00	235.00	1155.00	245.00	290.00	335.00
Pradesh	(2.31)	(3.74)	(7.32)	(7.79)	(21.12)	(64.83)	(21.78)	(223.01)	(568.81)	(165.89)	(230.00)	-	-	-	-
Assam	21.67	57.94	120.00	89.25	223.75	473.84	155.00	1115.00	2100.00	675.00	805.00	4662.00	960.00	1027.00	1051.00
	(28.0)	(63.15)	(132.24)	(87.12)	(198.41)	(428.63)	(159.73)	(279.79)	(2488.93)	(596.57)	(800.02)	-	-	-	-
Manipur	1.55	6.25	12.88	10.14	30.25	92.86	31.00	240.00	430.00	170.00	200.00	979.00	210.00	230.00	240.00
	(1.08)	(6.22)	(12.82)	(7.20)	(31.15)	(98.90)	(32.53)	(243.32)	(509.45)	(169.30)	NA	-	-	-	-
Meghalaya	-	-	-	-	30.00	89.53	33.00	235.00	440.00	175.00	210.00	1029.00	241.00	181.00	271.00
					(36.24)	(99.07)	(30.70)	(259.96)	(539.04)	(160.25)	(210.00)	-	-	-	-
Mizoram	-	-	-	-	NA	46.59	17.72	130.00	260.00	125.00	152.00	763.00	160.00	185.00	187.66
					(9.30)	(48.73)	(16.11)	(150.09)	(369.55)	-	NA	-	-	-	-
Nagaland	-	-	7.15	17.36	40.00	83.63	26.05	210.00	400.00	145.00	170.00	844.00	185.00	204.00	220.00
			(10.79)	(15.98)	(38.52)	(96.25)	(27.68)	(229.79)	(467.83)	(142.11)	NA	-	-	-	-
Tripura	1.62	9.41	15.51	11.44	34.66	69.68	28.00	245.00	440.00	200.00	227.00	1130.00	282.00	310.00	290.00
	(1.62)	(9.41)	(15.51)	(11.44)	(34.66)	(75.96)	(29.56)	(292.71)	(700.17)	(201.12)	(226.70)	-	-	-	-
NEC	-	-	-	-	0.33	0.00	47.00	340.00	675.00	202.00	219.50	1160.00	232.00	265.00	277.00
					(0.28)	86.60)	(32.66)	(385.34)	(779.80)	(196.95)	(218.93)	-	-	-	-

Note :- Figures in bracket are the expenditure. NA :-Not Available
Source :- Planning Commission.

Table 6.42
Plan Outlays (1993-94) FOR NER

(Rs. in Crores)

Sector	Arunachal Pradesh	Assam	Manipur	Meghalaya	Mizoram	Nagaland	Tripura	NEC
1	2	3	4	5	6	7	8	9
Agriculture & Allied Activities	39.60	139.33	23.60	44.74	26.27	23.60	62.90	3.68
Rural Development	9.27	52.10	4.55	9.75	33.99	23.85	17.40	-
Special Area Programmes	-	3.10	-	2.65	-	2.20	20:15	-
Irrigation & Flood Controls	16.30	92.50	49.90	11.85	2.94	4.20	21.00	-
Energy	41.80	226.00	40.20	45.35	28.21	26.89	42.30	120.99
Industries & Minerals	5.82	66.50	10.25	13.58	9.45	10.63	16.82	0.07
Transport & Communications	85.18	69.00	31.50	55.40	23.97	26.45	23.19	120.20
Science & Technology	0.18	2.25	1.10	1.10	0.43	0.36	0.90	-
General Economics Services	5.97	19.43	3.95	7.64	8.57	12.33	2.06	-
Social Services & Education	79.92	349.25	56.95	77.56	46.73	59.11	101.13	19.11
General Services	5.96	7.54	8.00	11.38	4.44	13.88	2.15	0.95
Total	290.00	1027.00	230.00	281.00	185.0	203.50	310.00	265.00

Source :- Planning Commission.

7

The Role of Technical Education in North-East India

In order to understand what role technical education plays in the economic growth of a region, it is necessary to envisage how it shapes the aims and implementation of economic goals. As has been pointed out in Chapter Four, fostering innovation and original thinking, helping to develop an ability in the creative use of knowledge, an ability for critical appraisal of results and developing an approach to problem solving seem to be desirable goals of technical education. However, such development of mental ability cannot be fostered by traditional teaching which is mainly concerned with the dissemination of knowledge. If technical education is to play a crucial role in the life of a nation, its content and teaching must both change. In this chapter some directions for such a change of content and approach are indicated.

One of the basic tools used for the planning of growth and development is the use of Manpower Surveys. Such Surveys project the manpower needs of the future and are supposed to form the basis of technical education. Such Surveys first of all assess the kind of industry adequate and required for a region. Based on this requirement, the kind and number of personnel needed is calculated. The existing institutions are then reviewed from this perspective. If necessary, additional and different kinds of institutions are proposed to fill the gaps revealed. An illustration of this kind is provided from the North Eastern region of India. However, neat studies of the kind mentioned above are rare, rather than the rule. But such planning seems essential. Table 7.1 shows the number of institutions imparting technical and vocational education of various kinds as on September 1992.

Between 1992 and 1997 the number in each category has gone up. For instance, there has been a proposal for setting up an engineering college in Manipur. A women's polytechnic has already been set up in that state. As for industrial training schools, nine separate institutions for women already exist in the region with a total of 544 seats. These were set up to augment the participation of women in the region in economic growth and to provide them with equitable opportunities for employment in various industries as well as in service sectors.

Table 7.1

Institutions	States						
	Arunachal Pradesh	Assam	Manipur	Meghalaya	Mizoram	Nagaland	Tripura
Engineering Colleges	-	3	-	-	-	-	1
Medical Colleges	-	3	1	-	-	-	-
Agricultural Colleges	-	2	1	-	-	1	-
Veterinery Colleges	-	1	-	-	-	-	-
Polytechnics	2	8	1	1	1	1	1
Technical & Industrial Schools	2	27	19	3	1	3	1
Teacher Training Colleges	-	9	3	1	1	1	1
Teacher Training Schools	-	33	1	10	2	4	2

Another illustration comes from the inauguration of an institute called the Indian Institute of Management Trade Wings in Shillong in May 1997. The purpose is to provide adequate training to local youth in marketable skills, in order to generate the right kind of motivation for participating in the process of development. A regional fishery college is also being set up in Tripura (IFP, Sept 20, 1997).

Changes are taking place in other levels as well. For instance, there has been a demand for a special Industrial plan for the North-East (Assam Tribune, 26 May, 1997). A separate forest policy for the north-eastern states is on the cards (Imphal Free Press, 15 Sept, 1997). The high level commission of experts on "transforming the north east" has recommended a series of steps to usher in socio-economic development in the region, which includes the restructuring of the North-Eastern Council (NEC) (Ibid).

However, one word of caution becomes necessary. If the requirements or needs are not assessed accurately, then the projections can go sadly awry and the nature and context of technical education can lose much of its relevance. For this reason the requirements need to be rooted in the ground reality and its overall perception. In this chapter an attempt has been made to identify and define the ground reality in the north-eastern states of India, keeping in mind the recent developments in the global context, so that such a perception can provide the input for manpower needs. The needs can then shape the form and content of technical education.

The overall picture presented in Chapter Six clearly indicates that the North-Eastern region lacks proper infrastructure by way of communication, water and electric supply as well as proper and adequate distribution of facilities of all kinds. As a result, proper utilisation of the abundant natural resources has not become possible.

How can this lacuna be removed ? It is here suggested that each region needs its own adequate planning of resources, in keeping with the distinctiveness of the region and its people. By its very nature then, developmental planning needs to be variable. This insight is coming to be increasingly recognised by the international agencies involved in developmental projects in developing countries. "Sustainable development" is now considered to be the goal rather than development per se. Thus development does not necessarily mean emulating the western way of life which has been responsible for degrading the land surface, water resources, atmosphere and its meteorology, and is leading to an ecologically untenable life style (Ghose 1996 : 50). Blindly following such a western model is likely to bring about ecological disaster. Moreover, any programme of change and development which neither involves the recipients nor grows out of their way of life, is likely to be counterproductive in the long run.

In the face of rapid ozone depletion, global warmings, the dismal climatic consequences like heavy rains and floods, deadly cyclones and typhoons, the rise in the level of sea water and the huge toll of life and property, the whole issue of industrial development all over the world, has to be examined anew. In the case of developing countries, the issue assumes even more vital importance as hindsight is now available as to the consequences of uncontrolled growth of industrialization. For instance, the steady loss of fresh water fish and the rise of carbon dioxide content in the Antarctic region are only two indicators of the rapidly approaching environmental disasters of the future. A recent report shows that there is an intolerably high level of pesticide residues in drinking water, dairy products and even baby foods in India (IFP, Sept 30, 1997).

Industrialized countries contribute 25 percent higher pollutants to the ecosystem than the rest of the nations. Such pollution takes place during the production of consumer goods and is a continuous process. The natural resources provide the input and are not replaceable. The process also generates an enormous amount of waste products of different categories, like solid wastes, effluents, gas and slag. Even the recycling of such waste results in the emission of different harmful gases. The entire cycle is thus an untenable one. First, it depletes resources. Second, it produces harmful residues which cannot be absorbed by the ecosystem. As a consequence, the delicate balance in the ecological environment is upset. As the WRI Report on World Resources 1994-95 pointed out,

> "Virtually all industrialised countries continue to release toxic materials, heavy metals, hazardous chemicals and acidic gases in enormous quantity and intensity. North's patterns of resources consumption are not environmentally sustainable either for the region itself or as a model for the world".
>
> ***(Quoted in Ghose, 1996 : 63)***

Two general points emerge from the scenario presented above. First, so far India has emulated the western model, beginning with the Science Policy Resolution of 1958 and following similar principles for its planning and allocation of finance. The second is that such a policy is not only unattainable but also harmful in various ways in the long run. Moreover, the social aspect of such plans have in general, not been considered in any systematic manner. The controversy concerning the well known Narmada Dam or the less known one regarding the construction of the Tipaimukh Dam in Manipur is indicative of such lacuna.

Principles of sustainable development and the inclusion of social factors in such plans have crucial implications for the planning of growth and development and for its application. It is in this area that technical education can play a significant role. As the earlier chapters have shown, technical education in India had, in principle, derived from its western concepts. With experience and hindsight, it can be seen to lead to an unsustainable utilisation of natural resources and wasteful practices. In the growing environment of ecological and social awareness and the search for sustainable growth and development, such a concept of technical education becomes unacceptable.

There is another drawback inherent in the policy for technical education in India. By its very nature, as a result of the various policy decisions, scientific and technical education in India is uniform in nature. However, the various regions of India are not uniform in nature. For different regions, differing aspects of development and change need to be focussed upon, presumably to suit the unique needs of the local environment, physical as well as social. Hence variations on the same theme do not appear to be appropriate. The burning need appears to be the restraining of the ecologically non-viable pattern of consumption and production followed in the industrialized countries. This calls for a drastic change in the content and methodology of technical education in India, specifically in the North-East.

In the following sections, some areas where such a change is crucial, will be indicated. In India, the rapid growth of population is seen as the main constraint on development. This works in two ways : first, the growth of population creates an immense pressure on the natural resources. Secondly, it necessitates intensified agricultural production. It thus appears that the objective of the country is to continue the process of steady and constant agricultural progress, prevent further degradation of the natural resource base and regulate the unsustainable pattern of population growth. These aims hold true for the North-Eastern region as well.

Since the north-east is predominantly rural in nature, land is one of the most important components of the life support system and the economy is predominantly agricultural. As has already been mentioned, land degradation, specially in the form of soil erosion, is the cause of many ills. As a result of erosion, dams, rivers and reservoirs gets silted, flows of rivers are impaired, resulting in annual floods, which destroy crops and lead to loss of life and property. Destruction of forests, shifting cultivation and construction of roads lead to a massive loss of top soil. This soil erosion can cause significant annual economic losses. Water logging and salinity of the soil reduce agricultural yield and cause further degradation of the soil. Water pollution leads to a loss of productivity and causes diseases. Poverty aggrevates the situation and sets up an unbreakable and vicious cycle.

Land degradation can be averted by the adoption of several measures in conjunction. The World Bank Report 1992 suggests that a "balanced management of soil moisture, nutrients and organic matter", coupled with practices such as "mulching, manuring, low tillage, contour cultivation and agro-forestry", result in the reduction of "surface run-off water, sedimentation loss and erosion by 50 per cent or more". Thus one of the important areas for strategies of environment management and agricultural progress seems to be the stabilisation of soil condition. In practice this calls for an overall different approach to flood management, use of fertilizers, afforestation and the like. Modern tools like remote sensing can be utilised for accurate micro-level surveys of various kinds. For organising and implementing such policy and practice, the nature of agricultural education has to change drastically. Such aims then will shape the content and methodology required for imparting the appropriate and adequate technical skills needed by the concerned personnel.

Forests of all categories play a major role in local hydrology and ecological protection as well as in the enrichment of the soil. They also serve as an effective carbon sink. A large part of the population, especially the poverty-stricken section, derives its sources of livelihood from forests. However, mounting demographic pressures lead to the rapid depletion of forest covers, which deprives not only the population of its only source of livelihood, but is also unable to support alternative land use. The added result is a further rapid erosion of top soil.

A different approach to forest managment, balancing socio-economic objectives of the people and considerations of ecological security for them, needs to be evolved. For such a step, first of all, social or agro-forestry need to be developed, so that the rising demand for food, fodder, timber and the necessities of daily life can be adequately met. Second, the requirements of raw materials for industry can be catered to by the proper development and utilisation of industrial foresty. China and South Korea for example, have successfully averted deforestation. But India's policy so far appears to echo the condition of the industrial countries in an earlier epoch. It is heartening to note that in September 1997, following the report of the S.P. Shukla Committee, efforts are on to draw up a separate forest policy for the entire North-Eastern region (IFP, September 15, 1997). It is hoped that the new policy will take into consideration the twin requirements of socio-economic development and ecological balance.

Another important resource for agriculture is water. According to Ghose, "A balanced and sustainable development process also calls for an economically viable and environmentally acceptable water conservation and management policy" (1996 : 76). For maintaining the productivity of land, sound management of water is a must. As has been evidenced, misuse and mismanagement of water resources of the country may lead to soil degradation and erosion. In India for example, the expansion of irrigation in the past forty years or so has led to an ultimate reduction of productivity. A global survey reveals that about 25 percent of all irrigated lands suffer from salinization as a direct result of irrigation practives. From that point of view, the lower extent of irrigation in the north eastern region of India, as shown in Table 6.3 might be considered a blessing in disguise.

However, this state of affairs does not rule out the need for a sound management of water resources. The abundant monsoon water of the north-east is lost in various ways : rapid deforestation leads to a surface run-off into rivers, and ultimately into the sea. It also means that water does not get absorbed into the soil, so that ground water cannot be repleted. Storage of water and passage of water flowing through the land need to be managed well, if this water is to be utilised maximally. Hence long-term programmes for water-conservation and management need to be framed. An assessment of different forms and qualities of water available and their use for different purposes needs to be made. At the operational level all these require technical skills and an overall strategy for managment. Such skills need to be imparted to technical personnel through technical education.

Water shortage is acute in many parts of the north-east. The ability to make the maximal use of what is available seasonally all through the year, needs to be learnt. It also requires educating the general public at the grass-roots level. Hence a part of technical education has to be concerned with propagating and disseminating such awareness.

It has aleready been mentioned how the earlier investments in irrigation in India over the last forty years have been counter productive in several ways. The growing extent of salinization and water logging hampering productivity has also been touched upon, drawing attention to the fact that the quality of irrigated lands deteriorated. The river valley projects built at tremendous socio-economic cost have not proved to be effective in the long run. Vast areas of rich forest were destroyed or innundated and a large number of people were displaced from their habitat and occupations. Heavy siltation reduced the storage capacity of the reservoirs. Emergency or distress discharge of water from the reservoirs result in recurrent floods and huge losses of life and property. So far no proper assessment of the socio-economic costs of such projects has been made. The time is ripe when the north-eastern region, rathern then following the models of Bhara and Champal projects for irrigation, and building huge or medium sized dams, adopts a more viable model, protecting the environment and its people.

For instance, water shed development, a unique device of saving 70-80 percent of rain water may be tried out in this region. This encompasses contour ploughing along the line of constant altitude, and the building of terraces and trenches in the hilly area. It stops soil erosion, provides water for irrigation and can act as an efficient barrier for flood control. The result is percolation of water into the earth and the maintaining of the water table. Compared to the big river valley projects, such a device has several advantages. First of all, it does not require a huge capital outlay or a very high level of technological skill. Hence local resources, both human and material, can be utilised, providing jobs to the local people at a much lower rate of economic outlay. The skills required do not need a long training time and can be imparted at a much lower cost. It does not destroy or disturb the environment and avoids the huge socio-economic cost of bigger projects. Hence the cost-effectiveness is immense.

In the agricultural process, usual improved agro-practices include the use of high-yielding variety of seeds for raising the yields per acre and the use of chemical fertilisers for increasing the nutrients in the soil. At the initial stages a large supply of nitrogeneous fertilizers is required. At later stages potassic and phosphate fertilizers are needed. The new variety of seeds is vulnerable to local pests and diseases, requiring the use of pesticides.

The use of chemical fertilizers over a long period of time leads to the degradation of the soil. The use of pesticides in an unplanned manner and in quantities in excess of safe limits affects the food chain and is passed off to humans causing diseases and defects of various kinds. In addition, such unregulated use leads to the development of resistant strains of pests.

The production of chemical fertilizers and pesticides require a large mobilization of resources and involves a high cost of production. Unable to do this, India imports a huge amount of fertilizers, causing a drain in its foreign exchange reserve. The installed plants release harmful pollutants into the atmosphere and entail huge costs for transportation.

Alternatives, cheaper and more eco-friendly, exist. An indiscriminate use of chemicals can be replaced by integrated pest management and bio-engineering of crop nutrients. The use of biofertilisers, vermicompost and the increasing application of organic manure, urban and rural compost, and farmyard manure can provide a cheaper and healthier input to agriculture. The extension of agro-forestry can provide green manure and preserve soil fertility.

The use of chemicals require prior accurate soil testing. For one thing, such facility is not easily accessible. Setting up of such facilities demand a huge personnel and financial outlay. Farmers become dependent upon government or semi-government agencies. But the use of bio-engineering overcomes such drawbacks.

Thus such measures can profitably be used in the north-eastern region. They entail an entirely different aim and approach for technical education. Such technical education is required not only for technical personnel, but needs also to be brought to the actual grass root workers. This envisages a restructuring of the system and a review of the content and methodology of such education. So far, English has been the language used as the vehicle for technical education. But if the education is to percolate to all, it is a moot question whether the mother tongue, the local or the regional language needs to become the vehicle or medium of communication. Brochures, pamphlets, reading materials, instructions, modes of operation need to be available in the language of the people concerned. There is a possibility of linking such technical education to adult education programmes.

The breakthrough in technical education, then, is envisaged to have two directions :

i) Use of alternative measures for development, which are cheaper, eco-friendly, less damaging to man and society and nearcr to the life style of the people involved.

ii) Developing those aspects of life and activities which enhance the quality of life and are a pre condition of development.

Examples of alternative measures in the area of land and water management and agricultural practices have already been provided. They call for innovation as regards to aims, priorities, methodology and training. It is in keeping with these that technical education has to be renovated and re-structured.

II

In the section that follows, attention will be drawn to those aspects within the existing scenario which need to be built up.

Basic industries require a massive investment and depend on two main facilities :

(i) Cheap and efficient transport and communication system

(ii) Easy availability of power

In the north-east transport is neither cheap nor adequate and efficient. The power situation is also not very promising inspite of the immense potential for power generation. Hence the setting up of basic industries in the north-eastern region does not seem to be a viable proposition.

On the other hand, consumer goods industries are labour intensive and require less capital. If the industry is rightly chosen, a good local market becomes guaranteed. However, it requires aggressive market strategies and the flexibility to adopt fast to changing tastes and time. From this perspective, two kinds of industry appear to be suitable for the area :

i) Essential (i.e. non-luxury) consumer durable and

ii) Agro-based products.

Essential consumer durables may include items like chappals, steel furniture, radio sets, ball point pens and other writing materials which are likely to be used by the larger section of the low income group (Bhattacharya : 1997).

Agro-based products could be those cash crops which require less capital investment and ensure a high margin of return. Spices and horticultural products provide two such possibilities (Ibid)..

The greatest possibility for rapid growth seems to exist in the service sectors in the north-east. In general. the growth of the serv ce sector is a good pointer of a developed economy. Such a sector is either non-existent or miniscule in size in the region. Services like man power recruitment agencies, courier services, advertising agencies and the like are concentrated in one or two big cities/towns and even these are not adequate either in terms of number, spread and efficiency. However, these are the areas where comparatively lower capital investment and human resource oriented development can change the nature of the existing infrastructure. Lack of faciliites of the most basic kind can be taken care of by such development. These will also generate employment outside the government sector which has reached saturation point in the north-east. Such development also provide scope for self employment.

This is the area where technical education can play a crucial role. Training for the service sector for providing service to the public at large at a reasonable cost could be one of the main thrusts of technical education in the region.

Technical education presumably aims to educate people for self dependence whether working for others or engaged in self entrepreunership. Hence, if technical education is seen as the instrument of social and economic change, then it must be relevant, viable and acceptable in nature. If earlier focus is to be changed, there must be an overall change at the policy making level. However, the thrust need not come from the top and filter down to the bottom. The necessities at the operational level may bring about changes at the higher levels. If that is to happen, technical education as it now exists needs to change its nature. An example of such a change has already been mentioned : the demand for a special industrial plan for the North-East. Such moves show an awareness and recognition of the gaps that exist in various sectors. There is also a general awareness that facilities for technical education that already exist,are meagre and do not serve the needs fully. As already mentioned, to rectify this, efforts are being made to increase the existing facilities.

In this chapter, several areas have been identified where scope for innovations exist. In fact, these are areas where innovation has become a crucial necessity. For such innovation technical education must play a crucial and significant role. This role has to be defined, planned and executed befor such changes can take place[1].

Notes :

1. The specification of such education requires another book.

Conclusion

In this book, in order to review the nature and role of technical education as an instrument of social and economic change, the issue of economic growth in material terms has been raised and questioned. The basic question has been : does more food, water, schools, hospitals, telephones, TV sets, electricity, scooters, cars, refrigerators, material comforts and entertainment constitute growth ? It has been suggested that such a perspctive is one-sided and ignores factors like social and ethnic identity, mindset and other social and cultural aspects. The unitary concept of development that has persisted so long ultimately leads to non-tenable or non-sustainable change. Hence the very concept of growth and development has to be looked at afresh. The role that technical education plays for such a change is crucial for the success or otherwise of the scheme.

The north-eastern region of India is in an unenviable position where its immense natural resources are being frittered away by following an unsustainable model of economic development, and where the states are unable to generate growth impulses from within. A seminar on the problems of development of Nagaland organized by the Naga Thinker's Forum, Kohima on May 26, 1982, found that for every rupee earned by a Naga, 87 paise came from the centre in the form of cash, subsidy, dole and other grants (Goswami, 1985). Without economic viability, no growth or development becomes possible. The right kind of technical education can and must contribute to such viability.

In a seminar paper Gurudas Das (1997) has pointed out various reasons for the failure of the region to mobilise resources. These include social, economic and political factors, of historical as well as of recent growth. For development then, all these factors have to be taken into consideration. This means that technical education cannot grow in isolation but has to be rooted in the context in which it has to operate.

Further, two approaches have been considered essential for a viable growth. Endogenous rather than exogeneous impulse is congenial to economic growth. In addition, there has to be a participating attitude towards the process. Technical education can not only show the way to endogenous growth, but can shape the attitude and approach for such activities.

Any programme for technical education then must take upon itself the task of promoting these two approaches if it is to be of any real use for contributing towards economic growth and development. In the north-eastern region of India, the available technical education, following a uniform pattern with the rest of India, cannot be of much use since neither of these approaches are envisaged within it. Whether the all India pattern should change is a moot question. But if technical education is to be viable,useful and relevant, it must set itself the task of identifying the reality and shape itself to face that reality.

Epilogue

While this book was being prepared for the press, several significant policy decisions relating to the overall development of the North-Eastern region of India have been announced by the Government at the centre. They reflect the awareness of policy makers of the special needs of the region and the need for a new direction in resource development and utilisation. Obviously such aims imply a constant change in the planning and implementation of technical education. Several State Government have also announced various damage - repairing measures and are actively considering the introduction of measures for changing the direction and nature of developmental growth. Constraints of time, however, have precluded the inclusion and elaboration of such recent developments.

Bibliography

Ashby, Eric 1966 : Universities : British, Indian, African. A Study in the Ecology of Higher Education. London : Weidenfield and Nicoloson

Ashby, Eric 1966a : Technology and the Academics. New York : Macmillan, St. Martin's Press.

Basic Statistics of North-Eastern Region 1995. Shillong : North Eastern Council, Ministry of Home Affairs.

Bearce, G. D. 1961 : British Attitudes towards India 1784-1858, London.

Bhattacharya, Debjyoti, 1997 : "Industrialisation and Impact of Liberalisation in India's North-East". Paper presented during the National Seminar on Liberalisation, Ethnic Identity and Economic Development of India's North-East, held at St. Anthony's College, Shillong. April 25-26, 1997. Unpublished.

Bligh, Donald, 1972 : What's the use of Lectures ? Harmondsworth : Penguin.

Bybee, Rodgers W. 1982 : "Historical Research in Science Education", *Journal of Research in Science Teaching* 19.1 :1-14.

Calcutta University Commission, 1917-19 : Reports in 13 Volumes. Calcutta 1919-20.

Collinson, G. Omani, 1974 : "Concept formation in a second language : A study of Ghanaian School Children." Harvard Educational Review 44.3 : 441-456.

Damodaran Committee Report : Report of the Special Committee on reorganisation and development of polytechnic education in India, 1970-71. New Delhi : Ministry of Education, GOJ, 1971.

Das, Gurudas 1997 : "Liberalisation and its likely implications for India's North-East" unpublished seminar paper, Shillong.

Datta, P.S. : Paradoxes of a periphery (understanding North-East). Land Reforms Unit. LBS National Academy of Administration, GOJ.

Datta, Sunanda 1986 : An Applied Linguistic Approach to English in Polytechnics in India. Unpublished Ph.D thesis.

GOJ Scientific Policy Resolution : No 131/cf/57. New Delhi, the 4th March, 1958.

Ghose, Chitra 1996 : Development Redefined : The Crisis of Sustaining Development, Vol. 1, Calcutta : Best Books.

Goswami, Atul 1985 : "Content of Economic Development in North-East India" in K.Alam ed. Planning in North East India, Guwahati : Omsons.

Hartog Report : Indian Statutory Commission, Interim report (1929). Delhi : Govt. of India Press, 1929.

Harty, Harald and Nasser, Al-Faleh 1983 : "Saudi Arabian Students' Chemistry achievements & Science attitude Stemming from lecture demonstration & small group teaching methods" *Journal of Research in Sc. Teaching* 20.9 : 861-866

Hewson, Mariane G. and Hewson, Peter W. 1993. : "Effect on instruction using students' prior knowledge and perceptual change stratagies on Science learning". *Journal of Research in Science Teaching* 20.8 : 731-744.

Ho, Kwok, K. 1982 : "Effect of language of instruction on Physics achievement". *Journal of Research in Science Teaching* 19.9 : 761-764

Huddersfield Conference 1966 : Education and Training of Technicians, Report of an Expert Conference.

Kothari Commission : Report of the Education Commission 1964-66. Ministry of Education, 1966.

Macaulay's Minute : Minute dated the 2nd Feb. 1835, by T.B. Macaulay, G.I.C.P.O. - No 1095 H.D.-19.7.78-25-W.B.G.

Macnamara, J. 1967 : "The effects of instruction in a weaker language".

Journal of Social Issues 23.2

Mallinson, G.G. 1947 : "The individual laboratory method compared with the lecture demonstration method in teaching general biology". *Science Education* 31 : 175

Noonan, J.A. and Mackey, W.F. 1953 : "An experiment in bilingual education" ELT 6.4 : 125-132.

Ogunniyi, M.B. 1982 : An Analysis of prospective Science teachers' understanding of the nature of Science". *Journal of Research in Science Teaching* 19.1 : 25-32.

Paranjpe, M.R. 1941 : Progress of education, Poona.

Pella, M.O. 1961 : "The laboratory and Science thinking *Science Teacher* 28 : 30-31.

Pella, M.O. and Sherman, J.A. 1969 : "A Comparison of two methods of utilising laboratory activities in teaching the course of IPS". *School Science and Mathematics* 69 : 303-314.

Postman, Neil and Weingartner, Charles 1971 : Teaching as a subversive activity. Harmondsworth : Penguin.

Radha Krishnan Commission : The Report of the University Education Commission (1948-1949), 2 Vols. Govt of India Press, Simla, 1950.

Sadler Commission (1917-1919) : See Calcutta University Commission.

Sargent Report : Post-War Eduational Development in India; Report by the Central Advisory Board of Education : January 1944. Delhi, 1944.

Stokes, Eric 1959 : The English Utilitarians and India, London.

Report of the Working Group on Technical Education and Vocational Training, 1960. New Delhi : Planning Commission.

Widdowson, H.G. 1979 : Explorations in Applied Linguistics. London : OUP.

Wood's Despatch : General Educational Despatch of 1854. No 49 dated 19th July 1854.

Wood's Report : Report on Vocational Education in India by A. Abbott; with a section on general education and administration by S.H. Wood. Delhi : Manager of Publications, 1937.

Index